Mavericks

Mavericks

15 Outstanding Stories of Extreme Jobs – with Exercises for Developing Reading Comprehension and Critical Thinking Skills

McGraw Hill Education

Bothell, WA • Chicago, IL • Columbus, OH • New York, NY

mheonline.com

 **Education**

Send all inquiries to:
McGraw-Hill Education
130 E. Randolph, Suite 400
Chicago, IL 60601

ISBN: 978-0-07-659069-8
MHID: 0-07-659069-0

Printed in the United States of America.

3 4 5 6 7 8 9 QDB 15 14 13 12

Contents

Unit One

Unit Two

Unit Three

To the Student

Can you name a person who thinks quickly and sees solutions where others see only problems? Do you know someone who weighs his or her skills against the risks and ignores the odds? You might call such a person a maverick. In this book you'll read about the special people, the risk takers, who work in extreme jobs that many people would never even consider. Need someone to defuse a bomb? If you don't call a maverick, you will probably wish you had. There's a pirate gang holding a cargo ship for ransom? Chances are you'll need a team of mavericks to bring them to justice.

For mavericks, quick thinking and problem solving are part of the everyday routine. Read *Mavericks* to see what it takes to report fast-breaking news from the front lines. Find out about the astronauts who repair the International Space Station—from the outside. Take a seat next to a bush pilot, hang with high-rise window washers, and get in the ring with ultimate fighters. Each article tells about a job that requires a high degree of mental toughness and determination. These are rough-and-ready jobs that can be performed only by mavericks.

As you read and enjoy these articles, you will also be developing your reading skills. *Mavericks* is for students who already read fairly well but who want to read faster and to increase their understanding of what they read. If you complete the 15 lessons—reading the articles and completing the exercises—you will surely increase your reading speed and improve your reading comprehension and critical thinking skills. Also, because these exercises include items of the types often found on state and national tests, you will find that learning how to complete them will prepare you for tests you may have to take in the future.

How to Use This Book

About the Book. *Mavericks* contains three units, each of which includes five lessons. Each lesson begins with an article about a unique event, person, or group. The article is followed by a group of four reading comprehension exercises and a set of three critical thinking exercises. The reading comprehension exercises will help you understand the article. The critical thinking exercises will help you think about what you have read and how it relates to your own experience.

At the end of each lesson, you will also have the opportunity to give your personal response to some aspect of the article and then to assess how well you understood what you read.

The Sample Lesson. Working through the sample lesson, the first lesson in the book, with your class or group will demonstrate how a lesson is organized. The sample lesson explains how to complete the exercises and score your answers. The correct answers for the sample exercises and sample scores are printed in lighter type. In some cases, explanations of the correct answers are given. The explanations will help you understand how to think through these question types.

If you have any questions about how to complete the exercises or score them, this is the time to get the answers.

Working Through Each Lesson. Begin each lesson by looking at the photographs and reading the captions. Before you read, predict what you think the article will be about. Then read the article.

Sometimes your teacher may decide to time your reading. Timing helps you keep track of and increase your reading speed. If you have been timed, enter your reading time in the box at the end of the article. Then use the Words-per-Minute Table to find your reading speed, and record your speed on the Reading Speed graph at the end of the unit.

Next, complete the Reading Comprehension and Critical Thinking exercises. The directions for each exercise will tell you how to mark your answers. When you have finished all four Reading Comprehension exercises, use the answer key provided by your teacher to check your work. Follow the directions after each exercise to find your score. Record your Reading Comprehension scores on the graph at the end of each unit. Then check your answers to the Author's Approach, Summarizing and Paraphrasing, and Critical Thinking exercises. Fill in the Critical Thinking chart at the end of each unit with your evaluation of your work and comments about your progress.

At the end of each unit you will also complete a Compare and Contrast chart. The completed chart will help you see what the articles have in common. It will also give you an opportunity to explore your own ideas about mavericks and extreme jobs and how the two always seem to go together.

Sample Lesson

Tornado Chasers

Eyes of the Storm

Storm chaser Eric Nguyen tracks a developing supercell thunderstorm in southwestern South Dakota, near the Montana border. Supercell thunderstorms are characterized by strong rotating winds that often develop into violent tornadoes.

It takes a special type of person to be a tornado chaser. Most people have no interest in seeing a tornado up close and personal. When they hear that death and destruction are headed their way, they either take cover immediately like Dorothy's family in *The Wizard of Oz* or drive as fast as they can in the opposite direction. Tornado chasers, however, live for just this moment. You might even see them jumping up and down in anticipation. For them, the bigger and nastier the approaching tornado is, the better it is. Fueled by adrenaline, they will actually drive *toward* the twister. Amateur tornado chasers do it for the thrill of the chase, but there are also scientists who chase tornadoes because it is necessary for their research.

2   A tornado is a vicious rotating column of air that extends down from a thunderstorm to the ground. Although small in size, with a lifespan measured in just minutes, an intense tornado will flatten almost any building in its path. You probably have seen photos or videos showing an entire neighborhood leveled by a tornado. Such total destruction is not uncommon. The strongest twisters pack winds of over 250 miles per hour. That is roughly twice the highest wind speed generated by a major hurricane. A tornado once lifted a motel sign in Oklahoma and dropped it 30 miles away in Arkansas! On average, about 800 tornadoes touch ground each year in the United States, killing 80 people and injuring another 1,500.

3   Tornadoes are nothing new, of course. But the idea of chasing them *is* new, dating back only to the mid-1950s. One of the earliest tornado chasers was David Hoadley. Known today as "the father of hobbyist storm chasing," he grew up in North Dakota and fell in love with the storms that frequently blow across the Great Plains. In 1977 Hoadley published the first journal for storm enthusiasts. It was called *Storm Track*. Another early pioneer was Neil B. Ward who, in 1961, radioed a detailed description about a tornado he was chasing to a local weather bureau in Oklahoma City. His firsthand information proved how valuable storm chasers could be to weather researchers. Ward went on to become a leading tornado research scientist, developing the first laboratory tornado simulator.

4   Both Hoadley and Ward were part-time storm chasers. The first full-time, professional storm chaser was Warren Faidley. He began pursuing violent storms as a newspaper photojournalist in the mid-1980s. Faidley gained international fame with an amazing photo showing a lightning bolt striking a light pole less than 400 feet away from him. When *Life* magazine published that photo in 1989, his career was launched. The text that accompanied the photo used the term "storm chaser" for the first time. Faidley went on to set up the first news, picture, and film agency that specialized solely in severe weather coverage.

5   Increased scientific interest in severe weather resulted in more sophisticated equipment. Scientists wanted to know why some thunderstorms produced tornadoes and others did not. One experimental device they used in the early 1980s was nicknamed TOTO after Dorothy's dog in *The Wizard of Oz*. TOTO was a 400-pound package of sensitive weather instruments

Tornado researchers practice putting a tornado data-collecting device in a storm path in Norman, Oklahoma.

in a protective shell. The goal was to place the package directly in the path of an approaching tornado. The tornado funnel would then suck TOTO up into it. The instruments would—the scientists hoped—collect vital data without being destroyed. This left one big problem: who would volunteer to put TOTO in place? After three years, the scientists realized that placing TOTO in the path of an unpredictable tornado was too dangerous. In addition, TOTO really didn't work. Only one tornado came close enough even to brush by it, and that one did not lift TOTO up.

6   Better results came when tornado chasers began using portable Doppler radar for close-up storm measurements. They mounted the radar on specially designed heavy duty trucks that could get really close to a tornado without being blown off the road. In 1999 one chase team got close enough to a twister in Oklahoma to measure its wind speed of 318 miles per hour—the fastest ever recorded.

7   Today there is a vehicle that can drive straight into a tornado if the winds do not exceed 150 miles an hour. This truck, called the Dominator, has bulletproof windows that can be pulled into place on top of its regular windows. It also has a steel-armored aerodynamic outer shell that can drop to the ground to prevent the wind

from getting underneath it. Finally, the Dominator has a roll cage like a race car just in case the tornado does flip it.

8   In 2009 Reed Timmer and two other scientists drove a Dominator into the path of what they thought would be a relatively weak tornado. When Timmer tried to lift up and latch the bulletproof glass, the window stuck. So he just rolled up the regular glass window in the truck and started to collect data. The tornado, however, was stronger than he realized, and the glass window soon shattered, sending broken shards flying into his face. Blood poured down his cheeks, but luckily the cuts were superficial and not life-threatening. Was he discouraged? Not in the least. "It might be risky," Timmer later said, "but documenting tornadoes at extremely close range is just what I love to do."

9   In 1996 the popular movie *Twister* hit the movie theaters. It sparked a tornado-chasing craze among ordinary people. This was exactly what David Hoadley had feared would happen someday. Hundreds of totally inexperienced men and women suddenly began showing up in the Great Plains to chase tornadoes. Even television stations started to compete with each other to see who could get the most dramatic film footage. The introduction of laptops, cell phones, and satellite receivers made instant storm data available to anyone.

10   These days, anyone can join the chase as a twister tourist. Resourceful entrepreneurs have established storm-chasing tours. For just a few thousand dollars, you can risk your life trolling up and down the Great Plains in a truck for a week or so looking for tornadoes. As one Internet tour site urges: "HURRY—seats are going fast for this season." Most tour groups, of course, are led by professional guides who vow to keep you at a safe distance from a whirling tornado. But for that much money, don't you want to get close enough to get a real thrill and have a story to tell your friends back home? On the other hand, are you really willing to risk ending up like Dorothy, wandering around in the land of Oz? ✳

If you have been timed while reading this article, enter your reading time below. Then turn to the Words-per-Minute Table on page 55 and look up your reading speed (words per minute). Enter your reading speed on the graph on page 56.

Reading Time: Sample Lesson

_____ : _____
  Minutes   *Seconds*

A Finding the Main Idea

One statement below expresses the main idea of the article. One statement is too general, or too broad. The other statement explains only part of the article; it is too narrow. Label the statements using the following key:

M—Main Idea   **B—Too Broad**   **N—Too Narrow**

___N___   1. Strong new vehicles such as the Dominator allow tornado chasers to get close to tornadoes safely. [This statement is true, but it is *too narrow*. It focuses on only one method of studying tornadoes.]

___M___   2. Scientists have invented various ways to get close to tornadoes safely to learn more about them, while amateurs chase tornadoes for the thrill and danger. [This statement is the *main idea*. It tells you that the article is about how and why people chase tornados.]

___B___   3. It is not surprising that tornado chasers are excited by tornadoes, since these storms are extremely powerful. [This statement is true, but it is *too broad*. It does not tell who tornado chasers are or why and how they do what they do.]

___15___ Score 15 points for a correct M answer.

___10___ Score 5 points for each correct B or N answer.

___25___ **Total Score**: Finding the Main Idea

B Recalling Facts

How well do you remember the facts in the article? Put an X in the box next to the answer that correctly completes each statement about the article.

1. The first tornado chasers began their work in the
    - ☐ a. 1920s.
    - ☒ b. 1950s.
    - ☐ c. 1980s.

2. The first full-time professional storm chaser was
    - ☒ a. Warren Faidley.
    - ☐ b. David Hoadley.
    - ☐ c. Neil B. Ward.

3. In order for TOTO to work, it had to be
    - ☐ a. placed on top of a telephone pole near a tornado.
    - ☐ b. driven into a tornado in an armored truck.
    - ☒ c. placed in the path of a tornado.

4. The fastest wind speed ever recorded in a tornado was
    - ☐ a. 150 miles per hour.
    - ☒ b. 318 miles per hour.
    - ☐ c. 520 miles per hour.

5. In 1996 a tornado-chasing craze began after many people
    - ☐ a. moved to the Great Plains.
    - ☐ b. saw photos of a terribly destructive tornado.
    - ☒ c. saw the movie *Twister*.

Score 5 points for each correct answer.

___25___ **Total Score**: Recalling Facts

C Making Inferences

When you combine your own experiences and information from a text to draw a conclusion that is not directly stated in that text, you are making an inference. Below are five statements that may or may not be inferences based on information in the article. Label the statements using the following key:

C—Correct Inference   **F—Faulty Inference**

___C___ 1. Most U.S. tornadoes strike in the Great Plains. [This is a *correct* inference. All the tornadoes mentioned touched down in Great Plains states, and the "twister tourism" is offered there, too.]

___C___ 2. Some scientists who study tornadoes have read about or seen *The Wizard of Oz*. [This is a *correct* inference. One package of weather instruments was nicknamed TOTO, after the dog in the book and movie.]

___F___ 3. Nobody ever photographed a tornado before 1989. [This is a *faulty* inference. 1989 was simply the year in which Warren Faidley's photo was published.]

___F___ 4. If you chase tornadoes with a paid guide, you can be sure you will be completely safe. [This is a *faulty* inference. No one can predict a tornado's path or strength.]

___C___ 5. Tornado chasers check the weather reports regularly. [This is a *correct* inference. They need to know where and when a tornado might strike.]

Score 5 points for each correct answer.

___25___ **Total Score**: Making Inferences

D Using Words Precisely

Each numbered sentence below contains an underlined word or phrase from the article. Following the sentence are three definitions. One definition is closest to the meaning of the underlined word. One definition is opposite or nearly opposite. Label those two definitions using the following key. Do not label the remaining definition.

C—Closest   **O—Opposite or Nearly Opposite**

1. That is roughly twice the highest wind speed <u>generated</u> by a major hurricane.
   ___C___ a. produced
   ___O___ b. destroyed
   _____ c. possible

2. Increased scientific interest in severe weather resulted in more <u>sophisticated</u> equipment.
   _____ a. famous
   ___C___ b. complicated
   ___O___ c. simple

3. The tornado, however, was stronger than he realized, and the glass window soon shattered, sending broken <u>shards</u> flying into his face.
   ___O___ a. yards of soft or silky material
   _____ b. sprays of wet, drenching rain
   ___C___ c. pieces of a hard or brittle substance

4. Blood poured down his cheeks, but luckily the cuts were <u>superficial</u> and not life-threatening.
   ___C___ a. on the surface only
   ___O___ b. deep within
   _____ c. extremely dangerous

5. Resourceful <u>entrepreneurs</u> have established storm-chasing tours.

_____ a. people who enjoy chasing storms, such as tornadoes

__C__ b. people who start and manage their own businesses

__O__ c. people who avoid work and responsibility

__15__ Score 3 points for each correct C answer.

__10__ Score 2 points for each correct O answer.

__25__ **Total Score**: Using Words Precisely

Enter the four total scores in the spaces below, and add them together to find your Reading Comprehension Score. Then record your score on the graph on page 57.

Score	Question Type	Sample Lesson
25	Finding the Main Idea	
25	Recalling Facts	
25	Making Inferences	
25	Using Words Precisely	
100	**Reading Comprehension Score**	

Author's Approach

Put an X in the box next to the correct answer.

1. The author uses the first paragraph of the article to

☒ a. describe the qualities of tornado chasers.

☐ b. describe the enormous power of tornadoes.

☐ c. compare professional and amateur tornado chasers.

2. What is the author's purpose in writing this article?

☐ a. to tell how tornadoes are formed

☒ b. to inform the reader about what tornado chasers do

☐ c. to persuade readers to sign up for guided tornado chases

3. What does the author imply by the statement "In 2009 Reed Timmer and two other scientists drove a Dominator into the path of what they thought would be a relatively weak tornado"?

☐ a. The scientists were used to taking chances in their research.

☒ b. The scientists had not estimated the power of the tornado correctly.

☐ c. The scientists did not have any experience with tornadoes.

__3__ Number of correct answers

Record your personal assessment of your work on the Critical Thinking Chart on page 58.

Summarizing and Paraphrasing

Put an X in the box next to the correct answer for question 1. Follow the directions provided for question 2.

1. Choose the best one-sentence paraphrase for the following sentence from the article: "On average, about 800 tornadoes touch ground each year in the United States, killing 80 people and injuring another 1,500."

☐ a. With around 800 tornadoes in the United States each year, the average tornado kills about 80 people and injures at least 1,500 others. [This paraphrase contains errors.]

☐ b. Each year, around 800 people are killed by 80 tornadoes, and 1,500 more people are injured. [This paraphrase contains errors.]

☒ c. Annually in the United States, roughly 800 tornadoes kill 80 people, and injuries caused by tornadoes number around 1,500. [This sentence correctly rephrases the sentence from the article.]

2. Complete the following one-sentence summary of the article using the lettered phrases from the phrase bank below. Write the letters on the lines.

Phrase Bank:
a. the history of storm chasing and some of its methods
b. a possible way in which readers could participate in tornado chasing for a price
c. descriptions of how tornado chasers feel about tornadoes and of what tornadoes are

The article, "Tornado Chasers" begins with __c__, goes on to describe __a__, and ends with __b__.

__2__ Number of correct answers

Record your personal assessment of your work on the Critical Thinking Chart on page 58.

Critical Thinking

Follow the directions provided for these questions.

1. For each statement below, write O if it expresses an opinion or write F if it expresses a fact.

__F__ a. Warren Faidley became known around the world in 1989 when his photo of a lightning bolt striking a pole was published. [This statement is a *fact* because it can be proved.]

__O__ b. The tornado is the most frightening kind of storm. [This statement is an *opinion*; it cannot be proved.]

__O__ c. Storm chasers should be paid quite well because the job is important and dangerous. [This statement is an *opinion* because it expresses a belief.]

2. Choose from the letters below to correctly complete the following statement. Write the letters on the lines.

In the article, __a__ and __c__ are alike because they were both part-time storm chasers.

a. Neil B. Ward
b. Warren Faidley
c. David Hoadley

3. Reread paragraph 9. Then choose from the letters below to correctly complete the following statement. Write the letters on the lines.

According to paragraph 9, in 1996 __b__ because __c__.

a. scientists began to use Doppler radar to gather data for their research
b. inexperienced people began to chase tornadoes
c. they were inspired by the movie *Twister*

4. In which paragraph did you find your information or details to answer question 2?

<u>   paragraph 4   </u>

<u> 4 </u> Number of correct answers

Record your personal assessment of your work on the Critical Thinking Chart on page 58.

Personal Response

Describe a time when you were caught in a bad storm.

[Try to recall your personal encounter with a strong storm.

Describe the storm and your reaction to it.]

Self-Assessment

Which concepts or ideas from the article were difficult to understand?

[Try to recall anything in the article that confused you or

prompted you to reread a section.]

Which were easy to understand?

[List a few concepts or facts that were easy to understand

and remember.]

Self-Assessment

To get the most out of the *Above & Beyond* series, you need to take charge of your own progress in improving your reading comprehension and critical thinking skills. Here are some of the features that help you work on those essential skills.

Reading Comprehension Exercises. Complete these exercises immediately after reading the article. They help you recall what you have read, understand the stated and implied main ideas, and add words to your working vocabulary.

Critical Thinking Skills Exercises. These exercises help you focus on the author's approach and purpose, recognize and generate summaries and paraphrases, and identify relationships between ideas.

Personal Response and Self-Assessment. Questions in this category help you relate the articles to your personal experience and give you the opportunity to evaluate your understanding of the information in that lesson.

Compare and Contrast Charts. At the end of each unit you will complete a Compare and Contrast chart. The completed chart helps you see what the articles have in common and gives you an opportunity to explore your own ideas about the topics discussed in the articles.

The Graphs. The graphs and charts at the end of each unit enable you to keep track of your progress. Check your graphs regularly with your teacher. Decide whether your progress is satisfactory or whether you need additional work on some skills. What types of exercises are you having difficulty with? Talk with your teacher about ways to work on the skills in which you need the most practice.

Bounty Hunters

Nowhere to Hide

Bob Burton is a highly respected bounty hunter who has brought thousands of fugitives to justice.

On March 10, 2007, federal authorities got some bad news. The electronic ankle monitor that Darli Velazquez-Armas was wearing signaled that he had not returned to his home as he was required to do. Velazquez was a Cuban drug trafficking suspect who was awaiting trial. Two weeks earlier, he had been released from custody on $1 million bail. Now, it seemed, he had disappeared. Investigators discovered that Velazquez had fled the United States in a private plane to the Dominican Republic. After that, the trail went cold. Was it possible that this alleged criminal would never be found?

2　　Law enforcement agencies definitely wanted to find Velazquez, but someone else wanted to find him even more. This other interested party was the bail bond company that put up the bail money for Velazquez. Here's how bail bond companies work: When someone is arrested and pleads not guilty to the crime, the judge sometimes lets the suspect stay out of jail until the trial date. In this case, the judge allows the suspect to pay bail money, which is returned when the suspect appears in court for trial. If the suspect cannot raise the bail money, he or she can pay 10 percent of the bail amount to a bail bond company. The company then pays the entire amount of the bail to the court. The court asked for $1 million in bail money for Velazquez. The family paid the bail bond company 10 percent, or $100,000. If Velazquez had appeared in court when he was supposed

to, the bail bond company would have gotten its $1 million back and would have kept the 10 percent as a fee. But Velazquez "jumped bail." The only way the bail bond company would see that $1 million again is to find the fugitive and return him to the authorities.

3　　To track down fugitives, bail bond companies turn to bounty hunters—individuals who, for a price, will do whatever is necessary to get the job done. (A bounty is a reward, usually paid by a government, for acts such as catching criminals and killing dangerous animals.) Bounty hunters have a dubious reputation. Some of their negative image comes from tales of the Wild West, where bounty hunters, armed with six-shooters, chased down outlaws who were "wanted dead or alive." Today's bounty hunters are more likely to use trickery or a can of pepper spray than lethal force. Still, bounty hunting is a risky business, and the job attracts an odd assortment of rough characters. Some of them don't always use legal methods. As bail bondsman Bobby Brown says, "You have to be really careful who you hire. You need to

make sure the person isn't just on a power trip."

4　　Domino Harvey was the kind of rough personality that is attracted to bounty hunting. A former fashion model and the daughter of a famous movie actor, she became notorious for her exploits as a Los Angeles bounty hunter. In fact, Harvey had her own problems with the police. In 2005, she was charged with drug dealing and was placed under house arrest. Several weeks later, she was found dead at the age of 35 from a drug overdose. Always unruly, Harvey liked the danger and uncertainty of being a bounty hunter. She used to say, "Heads you live and tails you die." Movie director Tony Scott, who made a movie about Domino Harvey, says

A bounty hunter takes O.J. Simpson into custody after the bail bondsman revoked Simpson's bond.

that, for her, there was nothing as intoxicating as kicking down a door to find out what was on the other side.

5   For the Darli Velazquez-Armas case, the bail bond company ignored risky characters like Harvey and hired Rolando Betancourt, a true professional and one of the most dedicated bounty hunters around. The first thing Betancourt had to do was figure out where Velazquez had gone after leaving the Dominican Republic. Betancourt began by putting together a team of investigators across several states. He also worked closely with government agencies, which is typical in such high-profile cases. Betancourt even rented a garbage truck and drove it to the fugitive's Miami neighborhood. He hoped that Velazquez's trash might contain some clues as to where he had headed. Betancourt didn't want to look suspicious, so he had to pick up the garbage from all the neighbors on the street. "It was a real smelly mess, but it had to be done," he said. Betancourt sifted through the stinking debris and found shredded credit card receipts and bank statements in Velazquez's trash. He and his investigators pieced them together and concluded that Velazquez had most likely flown to Spain.

6   Betancourt set up around-the-clock surveillance at several spots where he thought Velazquez might appear, and for a few weeks he came up empty handed. Then Betancourt got lucky. He learned that members of Velazquez's family had booked a flight to Madrid, Spain. Without hesitation, Betancourt bought himself a

ticket on the same flight. After landing, he instructed Spanish police to follow the family. The police trailed them to a house in the suburbs where Velazquez was hiding. However, when the police tried to arrest him, Velazquez broke away and sped off in his SUV. The police chased him, but Velazquez managed to get away.

7   Velazquez's escape made Betancourt even more determined to capture him. For weeks the bounty hunter searched, eventually figuring out that Velazquez was about to show up in Las Palmas in the Grand Canary Islands. Betancourt flew there and began searching across the city. After seven days and nearly 24-hour street surveillance, Betancourt remained confident. "I felt it was now only a matter of days or hours before I would run into him," Betancourt said. "We were breathing the same air."

8   At last, on August 9, Betancourt spotted Velazquez casually talking with someone on the street in Las Palmas. The fugitive had undergone facial surgery and had grown a mustache, but he didn't fool Betancourt. Still, the bounty hunter strolled by him once just to be certain. Then Betancourt alerted U.S. Embassy officials and the Spanish police, who rushed to the scene. Again, the cornered fugitive fled in a car, but this time he made the mistake of turning down a dead-end street. Velazquez abandoned his vehicle and began to run. Then he jumped onto the back of a passing truck. One of the Spanish police officers reached out, grabbed him, and pulled him to the ground. After

five months on the trail, Betancourt finally had his man. Darli Velazquez-Armas was placed under arrest.

9   Not all bounty hunters are as devoted and trustworthy as Rolando Betancourt. Some are more like Domino Harvey, skirting the edges of the law in both their personal and professional lives. Perhaps that is why some states, such as Illinois and Oregon, don't even allow bounty hunters to operate within their borders. Other states, such as Indiana and Nevada, require bounty hunters to get a license. In most states, however, anyone is allowed to make what is essentially a "citizen's arrest." You may collect a few broken bones and a bullet wound or two, but if you are the type of person who likes to break down doors to find out what's on the other side, maybe you have what it takes to be a bounty hunter. ✷

If you have been timed while reading this article, enter your reading time below. Then turn to the Words-per-Minute Table on page 55 and look up your reading speed (words per minute). Enter your reading speed on the graph on page 56.

Reading Time: Lesson 1

_____ : _____
Minutes   *Seconds*

A Finding the Main Idea

One statement below expresses the main idea of the article. One statement is too general, or too broad. The other statement explains only part of the article; it is too narrow. Label the statements using the following key:

M—Main Idea   **B—Too Broad**   **N—Too Narrow**

_____ 1. Some bounty hunters who hunt criminals are themselves unreliable law breakers.

_____ 2. Bounty hunters are individuals who will use any means necessary, legal or not, to capture fugitives from justice.

_____ 3. Bounty hunters are civilians, not police officers, who hunt for suspected criminals in order to earn rewards.

_____ Score 15 points for a correct M answer.

_____ Score 5 points for each correct B or N answer.

_____ **Total Score**: Finding the Main Idea

B Recalling Facts

How well do you remember the facts in the article? Put an X in the box next to the answer that correctly completes each statement about the article.

1. Darli Velazquez-Armas was originally from
   ☐ a. Cuba.
   ☐ b. the Dominican Republic.
   ☐ c. Spain.

2. A bounty hunter who had been a fashion model was
   ☐ a. Bobby Brown.
   ☐ b. Domino Harvey.
   ☐ c. Tony Scott.

3. Velazquez changed his appearance by
   ☐ a. wearing a hat.
   ☐ b. letting his hair grow long.
   ☐ c. growing a mustache.

4. Velazquez was finally captured in
   ☐ a. Miami.
   ☐ b. Spain.
   ☐ c. the Grand Canary Islands.

5. One of the states that does not allow bounty hunters to operate within its borders is
   ☐ a. Indiana.
   ☐ b. Illinois.
   ☐ c. Nevada.

Score 5 points for each correct answer.

_____ **Total Score**: Recalling Facts

C Making Inferences

When you combine your own experience and information from a text to draw a conclusion that is not directly stated in that text, you are making an inference. Below are five statements that may or may not be inferences based on information in the article. Label the statements using the following key:

C—Correct Inference   F—Faulty Inference

_____ 1. Bounty hunters have to be ready to travel anywhere in the world to capture a fugitive.

_____ 2. People who run bail bond companies are risk takers.

_____ 3. You can find out a lot about people by going through their trash.

_____ 4. It usually takes up to six months for a bounty hunter to catch a fugitive.

_____ 5. Although Betancourt put together a team of investigators, bounty hunters usually work alone.

> Score 5 points for each correct answer.
>
> _____ **Total Score**: Making Inferences

D Using Words Precisely

Each numbered sentence below contains an underlined word or phrase from the article. Following the sentence are three definitions. One definition is closest to the meaning of the underlined word. One definition is opposite or nearly opposite. Label those two definitions using the following key. Do not label the remaining definition.

C—Closest   O—Opposite or Nearly Opposite

1. Was it possible that this <u>alleged</u> criminal would never be found?

_____ a. suspected

_____ b. proven

_____ c. offensive

2. Bounty hunters have a <u>dubious</u> reputation.

_____ a. famous

_____ b. trustworthy

_____ c. less than honest

3. She became <u>notorious</u> for her exploits as a Los Angeles bounty hunter.

_____ a. respected

_____ b. feared

_____ c. well known for something bad

4. Always <u>unruly</u>, she liked the danger and uncertainty of being a bounty hunter.

_____ a. obedient

_____ b. difficult to control

_____ c. strange

5. Some bounty hunters <u>skirt</u> the edges of the law in both their personal and professional lives.

_____ a. stay close, but outside

_____ b. keep far away from

_____ c. break apart

_____ Score 3 points for each correct C answer.

_____ Score 2 points for each correct O answer.

_____ **Total Score**: Using Words Precisely

Enter the four total scores in the spaces below, and add them together to find your Reading Comprehension Score. Then record your score on the graph on page 57.

Score	Question Type	Lesson 1
_____	Finding the Main Idea	
_____	Recalling Facts	
_____	Making Inferences	
_____	Using Words Precisely	
_____	**Reading Comprehension Score**	

Author's Approach

Put an X in the box next to the correct answer.

1. The author uses the first sentence of the article to

☐ a. inform the reader about a big news story of March 10, 2007.

☐ b. catch the reader's attention.

☐ c. describe an unusual event.

2. From the statements below, choose the one that you believe the author would agree with.

☐ a. No bail should be set for as high as $1 million.

☐ b. Successful bounty hunters are tough people.

☐ c. Bail bond companies should rely on the police and not hire bounty hunters to catch bail jumpers.

3. The author tells this story mainly by

☐ a. explaining the risks that bounty hunters take.

☐ b. comparing the different styles of two bounty hunters.

☐ c. describing how one bounty hunter tracked down and caught a suspected criminal.

4. What does the author imply by saying "Some of their negative image comes from tales of the Wild West, where bounty hunters, armed with six-shooters, chased down outlaws who were 'wanted dead or alive'"?

☐ a. Bounty hunters in the Wild West were just as willing to kill fugitives as capture them alive.

☐ b. Bounty hunting began in the Wild West.

☐ c. The only law enforcement in the Wild West was provided by bounty hunters.

_____ Number of correct answers

Record your personal assessment of your work on the Critical Thinking Chart on page 58.

CRITICAL THINKING

Summarizing and Paraphrasing

Put an X in the box next to the correct answer for questions 1 and 2. Follow the directions provided for question 3.

1. Choose the best one-sentence paraphrase for the following sentence: "After that, the trail for Velazquez went cold."

☐ a. After that, Velazquez's hunters took a different route.

☐ b. After that, nobody knew where Velazquez went.

☐ c. After that, the weather turned too cold for the people looking for Velazquez.

2. Below are summaries of the article. Choose the summary that says all the most important things about the article but in the fewest words.

☐ a. Bounty hunters look for fugitives from justice, sometimes using rough methods. In his search for Darli Velazquez-Armas, Rolando Betancourt showed what a good bounty hunter does.

☐ b. Bounty hunter Rolando Betancourt searched for Darli Velazquez-Armas for months and finally caught him.

☐ c. Bounty hunting does not have a good reputation. Some states, including Indiana and Nevada, put restrictions on bounty hunters.

3. Reread paragraph 5 in the article. Below, write a summary of the paragraph in no more than 25 words.

_____

_____

_____

_____

Decide how to shorten the summary to 15 words or less. Write this summary below.

_____

_____

_____

_____ Number of correct answers

Record your personal assessment of your work on the Critical Thinking Chart on page 58.

Critical Thinking

Follow the directions provided for questions 1, 3, and 5. Put an X next to the correct answer for the other questions.

1. For each statement below, write O if it expresses an opinion or write F if it expresses a fact.

_____ a. Bounty hunters are violent and untrustworthy.

_____ b. Some states require bounty hunters to be licensed.

_____ c. Bail bond companies hire bounty hunters to track down fugitives.

2. Judging by how the bail bond company reacted in the Velazquez case, as described in this article, you can predict that

☐ a. the company will be eager to hire Betancourt again when it needs a bounty hunter.

☐ b. the company will never again pay a $1 million bail.

☐ c. the company will go out of business because it has lost too much money.

3. Choose from the letters below to correctly complete the following statement. Write the letters on the lines.

On the positive side, _____, but on the negative side, _____.

a. some suspected criminals flee before their trials

b. some bounty hunters act illegally

c. bounty hunters locate suspected criminals

4. From what the article told about Rolando Betancourt, you can conclude that he

☐ a. relies on luck in his searches for fugitives.

☐ b. dislikes bounty hunting but does it for the money.

☐ c. is a very thorough and persistent investigator.

5. Which paragraphs provide evidence that supports your answer to question 4?

_____

_____ Number of correct answers

Record your personal assessment of your work on the Critical Thinking Chart on page 58.

Personal Response

A question I would like answered by bounty hunter Rolando Betancourt is

_____

_____

_____

_____

Self-Assessment

The part I found most difficult to understand about the article was

_____

_____

_____

_____

_____

_____

_____

_____

_____

_____

CRITICAL THINKING

High-Rise Window Washers

A Bird's-Eye View

Two men clean the exterior windows of the 1,535-foot Oriental Pearl TV Tower in Shanghai, China.

On November 30, 2005, Hector Estrada and Oscar Gonzalez went to the roof of the 34-story Denver Place Plaza Tower in Denver, Colorado, and climbed onto their metal work platform. They lowered the platform down the outside of the building to the 12th floor and began to set up their window-washing apparatus. Suddenly, something went wrong. One of the supports that anchored the platform to the roof started to collapse. The platform plunged sharply downward. Estrada and Gonzalez were hanging on for dear life. Eyewitnesses testified that the platform became nearly vertical as it swung wickedly back and forth in winds that gusted up to 30 miles per hour.

2   Each time the swaying platform slammed into the building, it knocked out an office window or two. Eventually, it smashed about two dozen windows. Paper and debris floated out of the windows and began drifting like confetti before settling on the street. The street, littered with paper and broken glass, quickly took on the appearance of a disaster zone.

3   How long could Estrada and Gonzalez hold on to their platform? For nearly 15 terrifying minutes, they dangled in mid-air

while pedestrians on the street held their breath. "I was expecting to see two people die, and that was probably the scariest part," said one horrified eyewitness.

4   Firefighters rushed to the scene, but their rescue ladders reached up only to the 10th floor. Fortunately, Denver Fire Lieutenant Phil Champagne had a "Plan B." He ordered his men to rush up the interior stairs of the building until they got to the 12th floor. There, they cleared away the broken window glass and waited for the platform to swing toward them. When it did, Champagne's men used a hook to grab the platform and secure it to the side of the building. At the same time, they pulled the two window washers to safety. Estrada and Gonzalez suffered only minor injuries and did not even require a trip to the emergency room. In the risky world of high-rise window washers, they could count themselves among the very lucky. Neither one, however, wanted to test his luck again. The following week, both men quit their jobs.

5   Another window washer named Arturo Rodriguez was also fortunate to escape with his life. Rodriguez was a Mexican immigrant who moved to Canada in 2008. In 2010 he landed a job as a window washer. He was preparing to wash the windows of a 33-story Toronto condominium when he fell from the roof of the building. Rodriquez was saved from certain death only because he was wearing a safety harness. After free-falling 15 stories, he was stopped by the harness's

safety line. Still, he found himself hanging high above the ground with severe rope burns on his hands, drifting in and out of consciousness. Co-workers managed to rescue him by lowering him to a nearby ledge.

6   Rodriguez was only on his second day on the job when he fell, but even vast experience is no guarantee that things won't go tragically wrong. Take the case of Robert Domaszowec, age 49, whose father immigrated to the United States from Ukraine and found work as a window washer. The young Domaszowec learned the trade from his father. Yet, in 2008, Robert Domaszowec plunged to his death while washing windows on a 17-story building on Fifth Avenue in New York City. He had been washing windows on that particular building for 20 years.

7   To be sure, these accidents are relatively rare. Most window washers are not seriously injured or killed on the job. Even so, washing windows high above the ground is obviously a hazardous occupation. Even if you are extremely careful, all it takes is one slip, one backward step, or one loose rope.

8   Tracy Domaszowec said that her husband was always diligent

The weather is unpredictable in downtown Chicago, where winds can be very strong.

about safety. "He had yearly inspections of his equipment and always made sure that everything was in great shape. He never took his safety for granted at all." She went on to say, "People don't realize that being married to a window cleaner is very much like being married to a fireman or a policeman." In other words, when you kiss your loved one good-bye in the morning, you don't know for certain whether he or she will return at night. But if Domaszowec was so conscientious about safety, how did he fall? As usual, he had taken care to attach his safety harness to the bolts that secured the windows in place. With his feet braced on an outer ledge, he leaned out away from the building, expecting the bolts and the harness to support his weight. A police investigation, however, revealed that new windows had recently been installed in the apartment he was washing. Apparently these bolts were not securely set and could not hold his weight. Sometimes a window washer can take all the necessary precautions and still suffer a terrible fate.

9   Skyscraper window washing clearly is not for everyone, but the job does have its appeal for certain people. If you are the independent sort and want to be your own boss, you can start your own window washing business. Unlike many other professions, window washing has relatively few regulations outlining who can or cannot be a window washer. Also, in northern climates, window washing is seasonal work, which means you have winters off to do other things. So if you like to work outdoors and not have a supervisor looking over your shoulder, maybe this is the job for you. Of course, along with all that fresh air and elbow room, you also are exposed to the harsher elements—wind, rain, hail, and the sun. Of these, the greatest threat is wind because it can change so quickly, especially in congested urban areas where tall buildings create their own "wind canyons."

10   Window washing pays reasonably well. In almost every profession, as you move up the ladder of success, your salary increases with each additional rung. If you're a window washer, this is literally true—the higher you go "up the ladder," the more money you make. If you want to remain absolutely safe, you can stay on the ground and wash only windows on the first floor. If you want to make the really big bucks, however, you have to go up—way up. Window washers who work on the 60th floor earn a lot more money than those who work only on the 1st floor. The obvious reason is that they run a greater risk of having a fatal accident. For many window washers, the extra money is worth the risks. For Hector Estrada and Oscar Gonzalez, after their close call with death, the money will have to get a whole lot better. ✳

If you have been timed while reading this article, enter your reading time below. Then turn to the Words-per-Minute Table on page 55 and look up your reading speed (words per minute). Enter your reading speed on the graph on page 56.

Reading Time: Lesson 2

_____ : _____
Minutes   *Seconds*

A | Finding the Main Idea

One statement below expresses the main idea of the article. One statement is too general, or too broad. The other statement explains only part of the article; it is too narrow. Label the statements using the following key:

M—Main Idea   **B—Too Broad**   **N—Too Narrow**

_____ 1. Faulty equipment, bad weather, and bad luck often put the lives of high-rise window washers at risk.

_____ 2. Arturo Rodriguez is alive only because he was wearing a harness when he fell from the roof of a 33-story building.

_____ 3. High-rise window washing, like fire fighting and police work, is often a dangerous, even deadly, job.

_____ Score 15 points for a correct M answer.

_____ Score 5 points for each correct B or N answer.

_____ **Total Score**: Finding the Main Idea

B | Recalling Facts

How well do you remember the facts in the article? Put an X in the box next to the answer that correctly completes each statement about the article.

1. The platform that Hector Estrada and Oscar Gonzalez were working on plunged downward after
   - ☐ a. wind blew one of its supports off.
   - ☐ b. a rope connecting it to the roof broke.
   - ☐ c. one of its supports suddenly collapsed.

2. Hector Estrada and Oscar Gonzalez were saved after
   - ☐ a. firemen lowered the platform to the ground.
   - ☐ b. firemen secured the platform to the building.
   - ☐ c. co-workers lowered the platform to a nearby ledge.

3. On the day he fell, Arturo Rodriguez
   - ☐ a. had been on the job only two days.
   - ☐ b. was already an experienced window washer.
   - ☐ c. was washing windows on the 12th floor.

4. Robert Domaszowec learned how to wash windows from
   - ☐ a. his uncle.
   - ☐ b. his grandfather.
   - ☐ c. his father.

5. Washing higher windows pays more than washing first-floor windows because
   - ☐ a. windows at higher floors get dirtier.
   - ☐ b. washers could fall to their death from high floors.
   - ☐ c. high-rise window washers are union workers.

Score 5 points for each correct answer.

_____ **Total Score**: Recalling Facts

C Making Inferences

When you combine your own experiences and information from a text to draw a conclusion that is not directly stated in that text, you are making an inference. Below are five statements that may or may not be inferences based on information in the article. Label the statements using the following key:

C—Correct Inference   **F—Faulty Inference**

_____ 1. Workers inside the Denver Place Plaza Tower on November 30, 2005, probably didn't even know that the window washers outside were in trouble.

_____ 2. Hector Estrada and Oscar Gonzalez must have had strong arm muscles.

_____ 3. Arturo Rodriguez was working alone on the day of his fall.

_____ 4. The workers who installed the windows on the building from which Robert Domaszowec fell did not care at all about the safety of window washers.

_____ 5. After a window-washing accident occurs, people try to figure out why it happened.

Score 5 points for each correct answer.

_____ **Total Score**: Making Inferences

D Using Words Precisely

Each numbered sentence below contains an underlined word or phrase from the article. Following the sentence are three definitions. One definition is closest to the meaning of the underlined word. One definition is opposite or nearly opposite. Label those two definitions using the following key. Do not label the remaining definition.

C—Closest   **O—Opposite or Nearly Opposite**

1. Eyewitnesses <u>testified</u> that the platform became nearly vertical as it swung furiously back and forth in winds that gusted up to 30 miles per hour.

_____ a. denied

_____ b. guessed

_____ c. declared

2. He ordered his men to rush up the <u>interior</u> stairs of the building until they got to the 12th floor.

_____ a. outside

_____ b. inside

_____ c. nearest

3. Even so, washing windows high above the ground is obviously a <u>hazardous</u> occupation.

_____ a. risky

_____ b. profitable

_____ c. safe

4. Tracy Domaszowec said that her husband was always <u>diligent</u> about safety.

_____ a. careful and thorough

_____ b. careless and lazy

_____ c. intelligent and clever

5. Of these, the greatest threat is wind because it can change so quickly, especially in <u>congested</u> urban areas where tall buildings create their own "wind canyons."

_____ a. dirty

_____ b. crowded

_____ c. wide-open

_____ Score 3 points for each correct C answer.

_____ Score 2 points for each correct O answer.

_____ **Total Score**: Using Words Precisely

Enter the four total scores in the spaces below, and add them together to find your Reading Comprehension Score. Then record your score on the graph on page 57.

Score	Question Type	Lesson 2
_____	Finding the Main Idea	
_____	Recalling Facts	
_____	Making Inferences	
_____	Using Words Precisely	
_____	**Reading Comprehension Score**	

Author's Approach

Put an X in the box next to the correct answer.

1. The author uses the first sentence of the article to

☐ a. inform the reader about where and when one window-washing accident occurred.

☐ b. describe the qualities of high-rise window washers.

☐ c. compare high-rise window washing with other dangerous jobs, such as firefighting.

2. Choose the statement below that is the weakest argument for taking a job as a high-rise window washing.

☐ a. The job pays relatively well.

☐ b. The job allows the worker to be independent.

☐ c. The job can be quite dangerous.

3. The author probably wrote this article to

☐ a. persuade readers to be grateful to high-rise window washers.

☐ b. inform readers about the dangers and rewards of high-rise window washing.

☐ c. describe exactly how high-rise window washers do their job.

4. The author tells this story mainly by

☐ a. retelling his own personal experiences.

☐ b. using his imagination or creativity.

☐ c. describing several window-washing accidents.

_____ Number of correct answers

Record your personal assessment of your work on the Critical Thinking Chart on page 58.

CRITICAL THINKING

Summarizing and Paraphrasing

Put an X in the box next to the correct answer for questions 1 and 3. Follow the directions provided for question 2.

1. Read the statement from the article below. Then read the paraphrase of that statement. Choose the reason that best tells why the paraphrase does not say the same thing as the statement.

   Statement: So if you like to work outdoors and not have a supervisor looking over your shoulder, maybe this is the job for you.

   Paraphrase: Someone who prefers to work without having to report to a supervisor might like this job.

   ☐ a. Paraphrase says too much.

   ☐ b. Paraphrase doesn't say enough.

   ☐ c. Paraphrase doesn't agree with the statement.

2. Look for the important ideas and events in paragraphs 2 and 3. Summarize those paragraphs in one or two sentences.

   _____
   _____
   _____
   _____
   _____
   _____
   _____
   _____

3. Choose the sentence that correctly restates the following sentence from the article: "In almost every profession, as you move up the ladder of success, your salary increases with each additional rung."

   ☐ a. In most jobs, you make more money as you become more successful.

   ☐ b. In most professions, unless your salary increases, you are not successful.

   ☐ c. Climbing the rungs in a ladder usually makes you a more successful worker.

   _____ Number of correct answers

   Record your personal assessment of your work on the Critical Thinking Chart on page 58.

Critical Thinking

Put an X in the box next to the correct answer for questions 1 and 4. Follow the directions provided for the other questions.

1. From what the article told about the job of washing windows of high-rise buildings, you can predict that

   ☐ a. independent workers will continue to choose the job in spite of its risks.

   ☐ b. builders of high-rise buildings will design windows that can be washed from the inside.

   ☐ c. courts will rule that window washing is illegal because rescues are so dangerous and expensive.

2. Choose from the letters below to correctly complete the following statement. Write the letters on the lines.

   On the positive side, _____, but on the negative side, _____.

   a. window washers take great risks every day

   b. window washers earn a good salary

   c. some window washers work on the highest floors of tall buildings

CRITICAL THINKING

3. Think about cause-effect relationships in the article. Fill in the blanks in the cause-effect chart, drawing from the letters below.

Cause

_____

_____

Window bolts were not tightened.

Effect

He survived a fall.

They quit their jobs.

_____

a. Robert Domaszowec fell to his death.

b. Arturo Rodriguez put on his safety harness.

c. Hector Estrada and Oscar Gonzalez almost died.

4. If you were a high-rise window washer, how could you use the information in the article to stay safe and still get the job done?

☐ a. Refuse to wash windows on any day that is breezy, rainy, or very sunny.

☐ b. Make sure that bolts on the windows you are washing can support your weight.

☐ c. Work only with a partner who has more than 20 years of experience.

_____ Number of correct answers

Record your personal assessment of your work on the Critical Thinking Chart on page 58.

Personal Response

I wonder why

_____

_____

_____

_____

Self-Assessment

While reading the article, I found it easiest to

_____

_____

_____

_____

_____

_____

_____

_____

_____

CRITICAL THINKING

Humanitarian Aid Workers

Comfort Under Fire

Refugees wait to receive donated food distributed by the United Nations Relief and Works Agency in 2010.

It doesn't matter how strong you are or how noble your motives are. If you live in a war zone, there is a good chance that someone wants to make you a victim. That is the grim reality facing people who serve in combat areas to help those who have few resources to survive. These helpers are called humanitarian aid workers, and they go into regions of civil strife and unrest armed only with their special skills and good intentions. In the first decade of the 21st century, more than 700 aid workers have been killed serving people in Sudan, Iraq, and Afghanistan.

2   On October 12, 1999, humanitarian aid worker Kathleen Cravero almost met her death in Burundi, a small country in eastern Africa. At the time, Cravero was that country's United Nations Humanitarian Coordinator. She and several other aid workers had flown to a makeshift camp to deliver life-saving supplies to people displaced by civil war. When Cravero and her colleagues arrived, however, they were ambushed by a group of teenagers in tattered uniforms. The young soldiers confronted the group and then began shooting. Two aid workers fell to the ground. But then something happened to distract or alarm the young soldiers, and they turned and fled. This allowed Cravero and the three remaining workers to run into the hills. After 90 minutes, the exhausted group reached a small village where officials carried them to safety.

3   A person never gets over that kind of experience. But as horrific as Cravero's experience was, she was one of the lucky ones, because she escaped with her life. Zarema Sadulayeva and her husband, Alik Djabrailov, were less fortunate. In 2009 this newly married couple was in Chechnya, a region in southern Russia where government troops and rebel forces have waged a bloody war against each other for years. Sadulayeva and Djabrailov were working for Save the Generation, a charity designed to help children who had been traumatized by the violence. These two aid workers were careful not to take sides in the conflict. As one observer said, "There was no political element [to their work]. They just helped disabled children and children from poor families." Their work involved providing injured children with false limbs and emergency surgery as well as counseling. On the afternoon of August 10, a group of armed men burst into the offices of Save the Generation. Some of the men were dressed in black uniforms, and others were in civilian clothes. The men grabbed Sadulayeva and Djabrailov and dragged them away. The couple's bodies were found early the next morning.

4   The 2008 death of three International Rescue Committee (IRC) workers was equally shocking. The workers, two from Canada and one the United States, were in Afghanistan delivering relief to war victims there. "They were here helping Afghan

Karen Smith has helped to open schools and health clinics in Afghanistan.

people," said Canadian Prime Minister Stephen Harper. "They were not carrying weapons." On August 13, the three women were traveling in a white SUV that was clearly marked with IRC stickers. As their vehicle approached a small village, five men brandishing assault weapons appeared and began shooting at the IRC vehicle.

5   Stories like these might be enough to give anyone nightmares, and yet they apparently have not been enough to deter aid workers from carrying out their assignments. Despite the risks that go along with the job, humanitarian aid workers persist. They go on trying in their own altruistic way to make a positive difference in the world. One of these brave workers is a Californian named Karen Smith, who planned to pursue a career in breeding racehorses. A couple of years as a Peace Corps volunteer in Morocco changed her mind. She realized that the world had a much greater need for food and medical care than fast horses. So Smith became a humanitarian aid worker, moving from one hot spot to another. In 2006 she went to a remote region of Pakistan where an earthquake had leveled a school and killed 175 children. There she helped coordinate relief as well as rebuilding efforts. In 2007 she was in the Darfur region of Sudan helping to supply water and sanitation to some of the 96,000 refugees. Eventually, she was forced to leave that country because the Sudanese government accused her of spreading anti-government ideas. "When your name

starts getting mentioned in the paper," she later said, "it's time to leave." Smith then took an assignment in Afghanistan, helping to open schools and health clinics. She also worked to train midwives and set up literacy programs for the Afghan people. Within her first three months on the job, two huge suicide bomb attacks came close enough to rock the building where she was working.

6   Whenever Smith goes out into the countryside, she takes a security team with her. She also wears a bulletproof jacket and a helmet. "You do not for one minute take your security for granted," she says. On the other hand, Smith acknowledges, "You can't live in a constant state of fear. You just live with an awareness." The payoff for people like Karen Smith is not in the paycheck. It is in the small victories that come in the form of a child's smile or a simple "thank you." Says Smith, "I love my life and my work."

7   Out of the thousands of aid workers serving in needy areas, the numbers that are harmed by physical violence is small. Still, the risks that Smith and other humanitarian aid workers take by serving their fellow humans remains immense. One factor contributing to the danger is the fact that there is rarely any consequence for killing aid workers. Hardly anyone is ever caught or punished. Both sides in the armed conflict blame each other for the killings. Occasionally, if enough international pressure is applied, a government will promise to investigate, but the promise

seldom leads to arrests. Either the issue is quietly dropped or it drags on for months with no conclusive results. Because no harm comes to the killers, security expert Charles Rogers writes that the targeting of aid workers "is likely to accelerate in the years ahead." This may affect how aid organizations respond to some kinds of emergencies. If the situation in a particular country gets too dangerous, humanitarian organizations will pull out. The desperate and needy people there will no longer receive their help.

8   Humanitarian aid workers say they get immense satisfaction from helping others in need. But they do run incredible risks. What other job would require you to risk being killed for giving help to people in need? ✳

If you have been timed while reading this article, enter your reading time below. Then turn to the Words-per-Minute Table on page 55 and look up your reading speed (words per minute). Enter your reading speed on the graph on page 56.

Reading Time: Lesson 3

_____ : _____
Minutes   Seconds

A Finding the Main Idea

One statement below expresses the main idea of the article. One statement is too general, or too broad. The other statement explains only part of the article; it is too narrow. Label the statements using the following key:

M—Main Idea   **B—Too Broad**   **N—Too Narrow**

_____ 1. Hundreds of humanitarian aid workers have been killed in the first decade of the 21st century.

_____ 2. Humanitarian aid workers face danger every day to help the sick, injured, and needy in combat zones.

_____ 3. Humanitarian aid workers do an amazing job in countries all around the world.

_____ Score 15 points for a correct M answer.

_____ Score 5 points for each correct B or N answer.

_____ **Total Score**: Finding the Main Idea

B Recalling Facts

How well do you remember the facts in the article? Put an X in the box next to the answer that correctly completes each statement about the article.

1. Aid worker Kathleen Cravero was ambushed in
    ☐ a. Chechnya, a region in southern Russia.
    ☐ b. Burundi, a small country in eastern Africa.
    ☐ c. Afghanistan.

2. Aid workers Sadulayeva and Djabrailov were
    ☐ a. providing counseling and surgery to injured children.
    ☐ b. flying supplies into a war zone.
    ☐ c. protecting children by fighting off armed rebels.

3. Karen Smith left Darfur when
    ☐ a. the government turned against her.
    ☐ b. a bomb exploded near her workplace.
    ☐ c. teenagers waving weapons frightened her.

4. Most times, whenever an aid worker is killed,
    ☐ a. the killers are swiftly brought to justice.
    ☐ b. no one is caught or punished for the crime.
    ☐ c. people on both sides of the conflict come together.

5. When aid worker Karen Smith travels in Afghanistan,
    ☐ a. she travels only at night to stay hidden.
    ☐ b. she carries a rifle and plenty of ammunition.
    ☐ c. she wears protective clothing, such as a bulletproof jacket.

Score 5 points for each correct answer.

_____ **Total Score**: Recalling Facts

C Making Inferences

When you combine your own experiences and information from a text to draw a conclusion that is not directly stated in that text, you are making an inference. Below are five statements that may or may not be inferences based on information in the article. Label the statements using the following key:

C—Correct Inference   **F—Faulty Inference**

_____ 1. Most countries to which humanitarian aid workers go don't really want their help.

_____ 2. Humanitarian aid workers believe that their efforts make the world a better place.

_____ 3. If attackers had known that Sadulayeva and Djabrailov were trying to help children, they would not have killed them.

_____ 4. As long as aid workers stay neutral and don't carry weapons, they can be sure they will be safe.

_____ 5. In countries experiencing civil strife, it is often hard to know who is in charge and who is most powerful.

Score 5 points for each correct answer.

_____ **Total Score**: Making Inferences

D Using Words Precisely

Each numbered sentence below contains an underlined word or phrase from the article. Following the sentence are three definitions. One definition is closest to the meaning of the underlined word. One definition is opposite or nearly opposite. Label those two definitions using the following key. Do not label the remaining definition.

C—Closest   **O—Opposite or Nearly Opposite**

1. These helpers are called humanitarian aid workers, and they go into regions of civil <u>strife</u> and unrest armed only with their special skills and good intentions.

_____ a. discussions

_____ b. conflict

_____ c. peace

2. But as <u>horrific</u> as Cravero's experience was, she was one of the lucky ones, because she escaped with her life.

_____ a. wonderful

_____ b. terrifying

_____ c. surprising

3. Sadulayeva and Djabrailov were working for Save the Generation, a charity designed to help children who had been <u>traumatized</u> by the violence.

_____ a. wounded or distressed, often mentally

_____ b. taken away from home

_____ c. made healthier and happier

4. They go on trying in their own <u>altruistic</u> way to make a positive difference in the world.

_____ a. difficult to understand

_____ b. generous and caring

_____ c. selfish

5. Because no harm comes to the killers, security expert Charles Rogers writes that the targeting of aid workers "is likely to <u>accelerate</u> in the years ahead."

_____ a. slow down

_____ b. succeed

_____ c. speed up

_____ Score 3 points for each correct C answer.

_____ Score 2 points for each correct O answer.

_____ **Total Score**: Using Words Precisely

Enter the four total scores in the spaces below, and add them together to find your Reading Comprehension Score. Then record your score on the graph on page 57.

Score	Question Type	Lesson 3
_____	Finding the Main Idea	
_____	Recalling Facts	
_____	Making Inferences	
_____	Using Words Precisely	
_____	**Reading Comprehension Score**	

Author's Approach

Put an X in the box next to the correct answer.

1. The author uses the first sentence of the article to

☐ a. explain why aid workers love their jobs.

☐ b. compare the jobs of aid workers and soldiers.

☐ c. link the ideas of good intentions, war, and danger.

2. What is the author's purpose in writing this article?

☐ a. to persuade the reader to send money to aid workers

☐ b. to inform the reader about a noble but risky job

☐ c. to describe conflicts in several countries

3. Judging by statements from the article, "Humanitarian Aid Workers," you can conclude that the author wants the reader to think that

☐ a. aid workers are both caring and brave.

☐ b. kind deeds are always rewarded.

☐ c. no one can be trusted.

4. Choose the statement below that best describes the author's position in paragraph 3.

☐ a. Sadulayeva and Djabrailov did not realize they were in danger.

☐ b. Sadulayeva and Djabrailov did not understand the reasons for the conflict.

☐ c. Sadulayeva and Djabrailov did nothing to provoke the attack on them.

_____ Number of correct answers

Record your personal assessment of your work on the Critical Thinking Chart on page 58.

Summarizing and Paraphrasing

Follow the directions provided for questions 1 and 3. Put an X in the box next to the correct answer for question 2.

1. Complete the following one-sentence summary of the article using the lettered phrases from the phrase bank below. Write the letters on the lines.

Phrase Bank:
a. a warning that attacks on aid workers may increase
b. examples of aid workers who were frightened or killed
c. a brief account of what one aid worker has done in a series of assignments

The article "Humanitarian Aid Workers" begins with _____, goes on to describe _____, and ends with _____.

2. Read the statement about the article below. Then read the paraphrase of that statement. Choose the reason that best tells why the paraphrase does not say the same thing as the statement.

Statement: If those who attack aid workers are not found, arrested, and punished, attacks on workers are likely to increase.

Paraphrase: Those who attack aid workers must be punished, or else attacks will most likely become more frequent, and aid organizations will stop sending workers into countries where they could be hurt.

☐ a. Paraphrase says too much.
☐ b. Paraphrase doesn't say enough.
☐ c. Paraphrase doesn't agree with the statement.

3. Look for the important ideas and events in paragraphs 2 and 3. Summarize those paragraphs in one or two sentences.

_____

_____

_____

_____

_____ Number of correct answers

Record your personal assessment of your work on the Critical Thinking Chart on page 58.

Critical Thinking

Follow the directions provided for questions 1, 2, and 3. Put an X next to the correct answer for question 4.

1. For each statement below, write O if it expresses an opinion or write F if it expresses a fact.

_____ a. Humanitarian aid workers should not be sent to countries that don't protect them well.

_____ b. More than 700 aid workers have been killed in the first decade of the 21st century.

_____ c. Some countries don't deserve to have aid workers help them.

2. Choose from the letters below to correctly complete the following statement. Write the letters on the lines.

In the article, _____ and _____ are alike because they both accepted the risks of being aid workers.

a. Karen Smith
b. Stephen Harper
c. Kathleen Cravero

3. Reread paragraph 7. Then choose from the letters below to correctly complete the following statement. Write the letters on the lines.

According to paragraph 7, _____ because _____.

a. the killers of aid workers are rarely punished

b. number of aid workers harmed by violence is small

c. the attacks on aid workers are likely to increase

4. From what the article told about humanitarian aid workers, you can conclude that they

☐ a. are not at all concerned about their own safety.

☐ b. feel that the job they do is worth the risk.

☐ c. are not aware that they are putting their lives in danger.

_____ Number of correct answers

Record your personal assessment of your work on the Critical Thinking Chart on page 58.

Personal Response

I really can't understand how

_____

_____

_____

_____

Self-Assessment

One good question about this article that was not asked would be

_____

_____

_____

and the answer is

_____

_____

_____

_____

_____

_____

Secret Service Agents

Shield, Defend, Protect

Secret service agents keep a careful watch on spectators as they jog to keep up with President Bill Clinton.

On April 14, 1865, President Abraham Lincoln authorized the creation of the Secret Service. It was a tragic irony that Lincoln was assassinated that very same night, because today one of the primary missions of the Secret Service is to protect the president's life. However, Lincoln had no such goal in mind for the agency. Lincoln's main concern was to catch people who printed fake money since at that time, one-third to one-half of the U.S. currency in circulation was counterfeit. After the assassination of President William McKinley in 1901, the Secret Service assumed the full-time responsibility of shielding the president. Today's Secret Service agents don't stop there; they also protect the First Lady, the president's children, and the vice president. They also guard former presidents for 10 years after they leave office. Agents even protect major presidential candidates as well as certain foreign officials when they visit the United States.

2   Although that is a pretty long list of people needing protection, guarding the president remains the Secret Service's top priority. As one agent put it, "Our job is to maintain a 360-degree bubble around the president at all times." Agents accompany the president wherever he goes and for whatever reason, no matter if it's a morning jog or official business such as a campaign speech, rally, or overseas trip. If you ever see the president up close, look for the people nearby wearing earphones and looking a bit distracted. They are the Secret Service agents. And no, they are not really distracted; they are simply scanning the premises for the slightest sign of trouble or potential danger.

3   Being a Secret Service agent is a difficult and dangerous job. There always seems to be an individual who would like to harm the president, no matter who holds the office at any particular time. In this nation's short history, four presidents have been assassinated. Several other assassinations have been attempted but thwarted by the heroic actions of Secret Service agents. Being a Secret Service agent means putting the president's safety ahead of your own. To put it even more bluntly, you have to be willing to take a bullet for the president.

4   Clinton Hill is a prime example of that principle. He was a Secret Service agent in 1963 when President John F. Kennedy was shot and killed while riding in an open limousine in Dallas, Texas. On that day, Hill was riding in a follow-up car just behind the president's limousine. Suddenly a rifle shot rang out. "I jumped from the car, realizing that something was wrong, and ran to the presidential limousine," Hill later recalled. As the president collapsed, Hill saw Mrs. Kennedy trying to jump up out

First Lady Michelle Obama and her daughter Malia share a laugh under the heavy presence of the secret service.

of her seat. "I grabbed her and put her back in the back seat, crawled on top of the back seat and lay there. . . ." Hill said. As the limousine sped off for the hospital, Hill remained sprawled out, covering both the president and Mrs. Kennedy with his own body.

5 After that tragic day, the Secret Service tightened its rules about guarding the president. There would be no more open cars in a motorcade. All routes had to be planned and scouted in advance. Also, all windows and rooftops along the route were to be checked beforehand to ferret out potential snipers.

6 These new precautions may have helped, but they could not totally eliminate the dangers. On March 30, 1981, President Ronald Reagan was shot and badly wounded as he was leaving a hotel in Washington, D.C. Only emergency surgery saved his life. After President Reagan was shot, Secret Service agent Tim McCarthy stepped in and spread his arms and legs to protect the president. A reporter later asked McCarthy what made him do that when an ordinary person in that situation would have ducked for cover. "In the Secret Service, we're trained to cover and evacuate the president," McCarthy replied. "And to cover the president, you have to get as large as you can, rather than hitting the deck." He said his actions that day "probably had little to do with bravery and an awful lot to do with the reaction based upon the training." That may be, but McCarthy paid a price for doing his duty. One of the bullets fired by the would-be assassin hit McCarthy in the stomach. Luckily, McCarthy later made a full recovery.

7 Tim McCarthy was not the only hero in the Reagan assassination attempt. "It was a heck of a team effort out there that day," McCarthy later said. While he was shielding the president, another Secret Service agent tackled the gunman. Two others pushed President Reagan into the car, which then sped away. One of those who got Reagan into the car was agent Jerry Parr. He later said that saving the president that day was the culmination of his career. "All agents wait for moments like that," he said, "and when you really think about it deeply, that is where history, destiny hang in the balance. It is where all your training and truth come together. . . ."

8 After the assassination attempt on President Reagan, the Secret Service further strengthened security for the top executive. A president now rarely walks openly through a crowded hotel lobby the way Reagan did. Also, the Secret Service now asks that the president enter and leave hotels only through the parking garage and only after it has been fully secured. No matter how much security is tightened, however, some risks will always remain. The president is, after all, a public figure who cannot sequester himself for long. And so, as James Huse Jr., a former assistant director of the Secret Service, wrote in 2009, "There is no such thing as perfect security."

9 Clearly, the job of a Secret Service agent requires a person to have a certain type of personality. You have to be someone who can withstand extreme stress. You must be able to anticipate danger before it becomes apparent. Most importantly, perhaps, you have to react with split-second timing, not to protect yourself, but to put yourself in harm's way to protect someone else. That is an extraordinarily difficult thing to do — and yet Secret Service agents stand ready to do it at all times. "It is sort of like an invisible web of obligations that get inside of you," explained Jerry Parr when asked how agents develop that kind of courage and loyalty. "It is duty, it is honor, it is country." Finally, every Secret Service agent has to know that a thousand successes may be totally wiped away by a single failure. As one Secret Service official grimly acknowledged, "We clearly understand that there is absolutely no margin for error." ✳

If you have been timed while reading this article, enter your reading time below. Then turn to the Words-per-Minute Table on page 55 and look up your reading speed (words per minute). Enter your reading speed on the graph on page 56.

Reading Time: Lesson 4

_____ : _____

Minutes   *Seconds*

A Finding the Main Idea

One statement below expresses the main idea of the article. One statement is too general, or too broad. The other statement explains only part of the article; it is too narrow. Label the statements using the following key:

M—Main Idea **B—Too Broad** **N—Too Narrow**

_____ 1. The job of Secret Service agents — to protect leaders of our country and their families — requires bravery and loyalty.

_____ 2. Secret Service agents worked together to save President Reagan's life after he was shot.

_____ 3. Being a Secret Service agent is a difficult and dangerous job.

_____ Score 15 points for a correct M answer.

_____ Score 5 points for each correct B or N answer.

_____ **Total Score**: Finding the Main Idea

B Recalling Facts

How well do you remember the facts in the article? Put an X in the box next to the answer that correctly completes each statement about the article.

1. The Secret Service was authorized by
   ☐ a. President John Kennedy.
   ☐ b. President William McKinley.
   ☐ c. President Abraham Lincoln.

2. Secret Service agents are not responsible for protecting
   ☐ a. the vice president.
   ☐ b. members of Congress.
   ☐ c. the president's children.

3. The agent who protected Mrs. Kennedy was
   ☐ a. Clinton Hill.
   ☐ b. Tim McCarthy.
   ☐ c. Jerry Parr.

4. President Ronald Reagan was shot in
   ☐ a. Dallas, Texas.
   ☐ b. Washington, D.C.
   ☐ c. New York, New York.

5. After President Kennedy was assassinated, presidents could no longer
   ☐ a. walk openly in crowded hotel lobbies.
   ☐ b. ride in open cars.
   ☐ c. exit hotels through the front door.

Score 5 points for each correct answer.

_____ **Total Score**: Recalling Facts

C Making Inferences

When you combine your own experiences and information from a text to draw a conclusion that is not directly stated in that text, you are making an inference. Below are five statements that may or may not be inferences based on information in the article. Label the statements using the following key:

C—Correct Inference   **F—Faulty Inference**

_____ 1. Since the main job of the Secret Service is no longer to catch people who make fake money, counterfeiting must not be a problem.

_____ 2. Presidents are aware that there are people who would like to harm them.

_____ 3. President Kennedy would not have been assassinated during his ride through Dallas if he had not been riding in an open limousine.

_____ 4. There is nothing more the Secret Service can do to improve its ability to protect the president.

_____ 5. Secret Service agents check out alternate routes for the president just in case there is a problem with the planned route.

Score 5 points for each correct answer.

_____ **Total Score**: Making Inferences

D Using Words Precisely

Each numbered sentence below contains an underlined word or phrase from the article. Following the sentence are three definitions. One definition is closest to the meaning of the underlined word. One definition is opposite or nearly opposite. Label those two definitions using the following key. Do not label the remaining definition.

C—Closest   **O—Opposite or Nearly Opposite**

1. These new underlined precautions may have helped, but they could not totally eliminate the dangers.

_____ a. thoughtful plans

_____ b. careless actions

_____ c. big ideas

2. Saving the president was the underlined culmination of agent Jerry Parr's career.

_____ a. failure

_____ b. cancellation

_____ c. highest achievement

3. The president enters and leaves hotels through the parking garage after it has been fully underlined secured.

_____ a. emptied

_____ b. made safe

_____ c. endangered

4. The president is a public figure who cannot underlined sequester himself for long.

_____ a. reveal, mix with others

_____ b. withdraw from public view, isolate

_____ c. criticize, analyze

5. You must be able to anticipate danger before it becomes <u>apparent</u>.

_____ a. unknown

_____ b. close

_____ c. obvious

_____ Score 3 points for each correct C answer.

_____ Score 2 points for each correct O answer.

_____ **Total Score**: Using Words Precisely

Enter the four total scores in the spaces below, and add them together to find your Reading Comprehension Score. Then record your score on the graph on page 57.

Score	Question Type	Lesson 4
_____	Finding the Main Idea	
_____	Recalling Facts	
_____	Making Inferences	
_____	Using Words Precisely	
_____	**Reading Comprehension Score**	

Author's Approach

Put an X in the box next to the correct answer.

1. The main purpose of the first paragraph is to
   ☐ a. give a list of the people that the Secret Service protects.
   ☐ b. summarize the history and purpose of the Secret Service.
   ☐ c. describe the original goal of the Secret Service.

2. How is the author's purpose for writing the article expressed in paragraph 3?
   ☐ a. This paragraph describes what it means to be a Secret Service agent, stressing the fact that agents put the president's safety ahead of their own.
   ☐ b. This paragraph states that four presidents have been assassinated.
   ☐ c. This paragraph points out that there are always people who want to harm the president.

3. Which of the following quotes from the article best describes why Secret Service agents risk their own lives to protect the president?
   ☐ a. "There is no such thing as perfect security."
   ☐ b. "It is duty, it is honor, it is country."
   ☐ c. "We clearly understand that there is absolutely no margin for error."

_____ Number of correct answers

Record your personal assessment of your work on the Critical Thinking Chart on page 58.

Summarizing and Paraphrasing

Put an X in the box next to the correct answer for questions 1 and 2. Follow the directions provided for question 3.

1. Choose the best one-sentence paraphrase for the following sentence from the article: "You have to be someone who can withstand extreme stress."

☐ a. You need to be able to handle physical and mental pressures.

☐ b. It is extremely important that you are not a tense person.

☐ c. Most people have trouble dealing with stress.

2. Below are summaries of the article. Choose the summary that says all the most important things about the article but in the fewest words.

☐ a. Secret Service agents have the dangerous job of protecting the president.

☐ b. Although the original job of the Secret Service was catching counterfeiters, its primary goal has changed to protecting the president. Over the years, many agents have risked their lives to carry out this mission.

☐ c. The Secret Service dates from the time of President Lincoln. Agents are supposed to protect the president, but despite their best efforts, Presidents Kennedy and Reagan were shot.

3. Look for the important ideas and events in paragraphs 4 and 5. Summarize those paragraphs in one or two sentences.

_____

_____

_____

_____

_____ Number of correct answers

Record your personal assessment of your work on the Critical Thinking Chart on page 58.

Critical Thinking

Put an X in the box next to the correct answer for questions 1 and 4. Follow the directions provided for the other questions.

1. From the information in paragraphs 5 and 8, you can predict that the Secret Service

☐ a. will never need to make any more changes in the way its agents guard the president.

☐ b. will make their rules about guarding the president less strict.

☐ c. will make whatever changes are needed to guard the president.

2. Choose from the letters below to correctly complete the following statement. Write the letters on the lines.

In the article, _____ and _____ are different.

a. the actions of some brave Secret Service agents

b. the purpose of the Secret Service today

c. the original goal of the Secret Service

3. Choose from the letters below to correctly complete the following statement. Write the letters on the lines.

According to the article, _____, which caused agent Tim McCarthy to

_____, and the effect was that_____.

a. a would-be assassin shot at President Reagan

b. the agent was shot in the stomach

c. spread his arms and legs to protect the president

4. From the information in the last paragraph, you can conclude that

☐ a. Secret Service agents do not have a sense of fear.

☐ b. not many people would want to be Secret Service agents.

☐ c. applicants must meet very high standards in order to become Secret Service agents.

5. In which paragraph did you find the information for your answer to question 3?

_____

_____ Number of correct answers

Record your personal assessment of your work on the Critical Thinking Chart on page 58.

Personal Response

What was most surprising or interesting to you about this article?

_____

_____

_____

Self-Assessment

Before reading this article, I already knew

_____

_____

_____

_____

_____

_____

_____

_____

Tiger Trainers
Schooling the Big Cats

White Bengal tigers are an endangered species and are rarely found in the wild. Most live in protected wild game preserves or in zoos.

At first glance, being a tiger trainer may seem like something anyone can do. You don't need a college degree—in fact, you don't need a degree of any kind. You don't need computer skills, math skills, musical ability, or foreign-language training. It does not matter if you are tall or short, male or female, big or little. Whoever and whatever you are, you can make lots of money—or maybe even become famous—by coaxing a tiger to leap through a hoop or encouraging it to curl up at your feet.

2 Chao Gaimin, one of the most famous tiger trainers in China, is living proof of this. Growing up in rural China, Chao could not have foreseen her future as a professional tiger tamer. She was born into a poor family, dropped out of school at age 14, and eked out a living as a migrant worker for two years before taking a job at a local zoo. Two months later she was training Manchurian tigers.

3 Working with wild roaring animals may sound like a cool job to you, but there are some important things to know. For starters, there is no shortcut to success. Chao's experience was the exception, rather than the rule. Most people can expect to spend 10 years or more learning on the job. The first couple of years you probably won't even get close to a big cat, but you will be able to clean their cages. If you are good at that, you could move up to the job of "back-up" or apprentice trainer. Diane Guerrero, a professional animal trainer, says the back-up trainer is the person who manages the crowd and alerts the trainer to possible problems or obstacles. "They handle everything else but the animal!" she says. However, the back-up quickly is called into duty to assist the trainer if any trouble occurs.

4 Not only will your days as a back-up have lots of routine and little glory, they will also be extremely long. You will most likely be expected to work all day, every day. At one training center for big cats in the United States, apprentice trainers are expected to work around the clock 365 days a year. That means you get no time off at the holidays, no weekends, and no vacations at all. By taking a job as an apprentice animal trainer you are essentially going off to boot camp. As one job posting bluntly states, "Plan on being here every day for at least two years without leaving."

5 There is a reason for this intensity. You need to be around tigers—you need to log literally thousands of hours around them— before you can begin to understand them. Says Diane Guerrero, "You essentially have to become one with the animal to understand how they think, react, and feel." Trainer Chris Heiden agrees, declaring that it "takes every moment of every day for you to observe and experience the animals." This understanding will pay off when you actually begin to train the animals. Chao Garmin says that after years spent with tigers, she can read their moods just by looking at them. "If they're happy, they'll let their tongues hang out and narrow their eyes," she says. "And if they feel lonely, they murmur at night and gaze into the distance with a look of longing."

6 When you begin the actual training, there are a variety of approaches you might use. Many big cat trainers use operant conditioning, a system of positive and negative rewards and punishments that shape the animal's behavior. The idea is to

A male Bengal tiger can grow up to 10 feet long, from nose to tail, and weigh 500 pounds.

have the creature form an association between a behavior and a consequence. For example, the animal learns that if it lies down when a specific command is given, it will receive a treat. Tiger trainer Roy Horn, of the famous *Siegfried and Roy Show*, used a different technique. Horn called it "affection conditioning." It involved giving tigers his constant love and affection from the time they were born, even letting them sleep with him until they were a year old. Chilean tiger trainer Tabayara Maluenda uses a combination of rewards and affection. He calls his technique "loving reinforcement," saying some of his tigers respond better to a gentle touch, while others do best with rewards they can eat.

7   Whatever technique you choose, you'd be wise to keep in mind that just because a tiger can be trained, that doesn't mean it is tamed. These majestic felines will always retain the instincts and proclivities of a predator. Declares trainer Bhagavan Antle, "Many cats are very nice when they are young, but may become killers as they mature, no matter how you treat them."

8   There are plenty of examples in just recent history. In 2006 an experienced trainer at the San Francisco Zoo was mauled during a routine feeding of a tiger. In 2007 a tiger critically injured its caretaker while the man was cleaning its cage. In 2009, three tigers pounced on

trainer Christian Walliser when he tripped during a circus act with them. "They were on him in an instant," said one witness. Walliser survived, but just barely.

9   The same is true for Roy Horn, probably the most famous tiger trainer to fall victim to a trained cat. Roy was performing in Las Vegas in front of a packed house, something he had done thousands of times before. As part of the show, he brought out a 380-pound white tiger. As Roy began leading the cat through its variety of tricks, someone or something in the crowd distracted the animal. Roy stepped forward to regain the tiger's attention, commanding it to lie down. The beast did not respond, so Roy tried to grab the tiger's collar. At that point, the animal grabbed Roy's wrist with its paw.

10   "Release!" shouted Roy, trying to pull away. "Release!"

11   The tiger obeyed, letting go so suddenly that Roy fell backward. Instantly the tiger leaped forward, sinking its teeth into Roy's neck and dragging him off stage. By the time Roy could be rushed to the hospital for emergency surgery, he had lost massive amounts of blood. For days, he remained in critical condition. Although he did survive, it took him years to recover.

12   Some trainers believe that the white tiger was actually trying to protect Roy by dragging him off by the scruff of his neck,

as it would a cub, without intending to hurt him. Others maintain that any tiger will attack when it sees a living being fall down. Trainer Kay Rosaire believes the tiger just reacted on instinct. "They're predators, so who can really know what goes on in their minds?"

13   If you still think training tigers is a cool job, then perhaps this really is the career for you. Just don't make the mistake a few trainers have made. The big kitty that does what you say may *seem* friendly, but don't fall down on the job—or you may find you are more feast than friend. ✳

If you have been timed while reading this article, enter your reading time below. Then turn to the Words-per-Minute Table on page 55 and look up your reading speed (words per minute). Enter your reading speed on the graph on page 56.

Reading Time: **Lesson 5**

_____ : _____
   Minutes   *Seconds*

A Finding the Main Idea

One statement below expresses the main idea of the article. One statement is too general, or too broad. The other statement explains only part of the article; it is too narrow. Label the statements using the following key:

M—Main Idea   **B—Too Broad**   **N—Too Narrow**

_____ 1. Most would-be tiger trainers should expect to go through a training period of around 10 years.

_____ 2. Although tiger trainers spend years learning how to handle tigers, they still face danger, since tigers are wild animals.

_____ 3. If you want a safe and predictable job, tiger training is probably not the right career for you.

_____ Score 15 points for a correct M answer.

_____ Score 5 points for each correct B or N answer.

_____ **Total Score:** Finding the Main Idea

B Recalling Facts

How well do you remember the facts in the article? Put an X in the box next to the answer that correctly completes each statement about the article.

1. An apprentice trainer
   ☐ a. cleans the tiger's cage every day.
   ☐ b. handles the tiger together with the tiger trainer.
   ☐ c. manages the crowd and alerts the trainer to problems.

2. Chao Garmin says she knows a tiger is happy if it
   ☐ a. growls deep in its throat.
   ☐ b. murmurs at night.
   ☐ c. narrows its eyes.

3. A tiger trainer who uses operant conditioning
   ☐ a. sleeps with a tiger when it is young.
   ☐ b. rewards a tiger for good behavior.
   ☐ c. combines a gentle touch with punishment.

4. Christian Walliser was attacked by tigers
   ☐ a. when he tripped and fell during a circus act.
   ☐ b. as he was cleaning the tiger cage.
   ☐ c. during a routine tiger feeding.

5. A tiger dragged trainer Roy Horn off stage after Roy
   ☐ a. fell down in front of the tiger.
   ☐ b. hit the tiger with a whip.
   ☐ c. turned his back on the tiger.

Score 5 points for each correct answer.

_____ **Total Score:** Recalling Facts

C Making Inferences

When you combine your own experiences and information from a text to draw a conclusion that is not directly stated in that text, you are making an inference. Below are five statements that may or may not be inferences based on information in the article. Label the statements using the following key:

C—Correct Inference   **F—Faulty Inference**

_____ 1. Everyone, including even Chao Gaimin, was amazed at how quickly she developed the skill it takes to be a professional tiger trainer.

_____ 2. An experienced tiger trainer would have no trouble training another large animal.

_____ 3. Most spectators at Roy Horn's show thought the tiger attack was part of the act until the emergency vehicles took Horn away.

_____ 4. It is a rare person who has the patience and dedication to become a tiger trainer.

_____ 5. Many tiger trainers, even after they are attacked by tigers, still love and admire the animals.

> Score 5 points for each correct answer.
>
> _____ **Total Score**: Making Inferences

D Using Words Precisely

Each numbered sentence below contains an underlined word or phrase from the article. Following the sentence are three definitions. One definition is closest to the meaning of the underlined word. One definition is opposite or nearly opposite. Label those two definitions using the following key. Do not label the remaining definition.

C—Closest   **O—Opposite or Nearly Opposite**

1. She was born into a poor family, dropped out of school at age 14, and eked out a living as a <u>migrant</u> worker for two years before taking a job at a local zoo.

_____ a. poorly paid

_____ b. moving from place to place

_____ c. staying in one place

2. As one job posting <u>bluntly</u> states, "Plan on being here every day for at least two years without leaving."

_____ a. honestly, but abruptly

_____ b. tricky and confusing

_____ c. later than expected

3. The idea is to have the creature form an association between a behavior and a <u>consequence</u>.

_____ a. an action that causes a certain effect

_____ b. something that follows naturally after an action

_____ c. feeling of regret for a past action

4. These majestic felines will always retain the instincts and <u>proclivities</u> of a predator.

_____ a. unusual behavior

_____ b. memories

_____ c. natural preferences

5. In 2006 an experienced trainer at the San Francisco Zoo was <u>mauled</u> during a routine feeding of a tiger.

_____ a. surprised

_____ b. handled gently

_____ c. battered

_____ Score 3 points for each correct C answer.

_____ Score 2 points for each correct O answer.

_____ **Total Score**: Using Words Precisely

Enter the four total scores in the spaces below, and add them together to find your Reading Comprehension Score. Then record your score on the graph on page 57.

Score	Question Type	Lesson 5
_____	Finding the Main Idea	
_____	Recalling Facts	
_____	Making Inferences	
_____	Using Words Precisely	
_____	**Reading Comprehension Score**	

Author's Approach

Put an X in the box next to the correct answer.

1. The main purpose of the first paragraph is to
   ☐ a. suggest that being a tiger trainer may not be as easy as it seems at first.
   ☐ b. describe all the tricks that a tiger does for its trainer.
   ☐ c. describe the training it takes to become a tiger trainer.

2. What is the author's purpose in writing this article?
   ☐ a. to get the reader to consider becoming a tiger trainer
   ☐ b. to tell what happens when tigers turn on their trainers
   ☐ c. to describe what it takes to be a tiger trainer

3. From the statements below, choose the one that you believe the author would agree with.
   ☐ a. Training tigers is a reckless waste of time.
   ☐ b. Training tigers takes skill, patience, and courage.
   ☐ c. Training tigers is actually a pretty easy job.

4. What does the author mean by the statement "By taking a job as an apprentice animal trainer, you are essentially going off to boot camp"?
   ☐ a. Apprentice animal training is sure to lead to a good career.
   ☐ b. Apprentice training, like military training, is difficult.
   ☐ c. The things you have to do in apprentice animal training could get you killed.

_____ Number of correct answers

Record your personal assessment of your work on the Critical Thinking Chart on page 58.

Summarizing and Paraphrasing

Follow the directions provided for questions 1 and 2. Put an X in the box next to the correct answer for question 3.

1. Complete the following one-sentence summary of the article using the lettered phrases from the phrase bank below. Write the letters on the lines.

> **Phrase Bank:**
> a. various techniques for tiger training
> b. how tiger trainers prepare for the job
> c. examples of times when tigers attacked trainers

The article, "Tiger Trainers: Schooling the Big Cats" begins with _____, goes on to describe _____, and ends with _____.

2. Look for the important ideas and events in paragraphs 3 and 4. Summarize those paragraphs in one or two sentences.

_____

_____

_____

_____

3. Choose the sentence that correctly restates the following sentence from the article: "Chao's experience was the exception rather than the rule."

☐ a. Chao wanted to break all the rules.

☐ b. What Chao did was against the rules.

☐ c. What Chao experienced was unusual.

_____ Number of correct answers

Record your personal assessment of your work on the Critical Thinking Chart on page 58.

Critical Thinking

Follow the directions provided for questions 1, 3 and 4. Put an X next to the correct answer for questions 2 and 5.

1. For each statement below, write O if it expresses an opinion or write F if it expresses a fact.

_____ a. Apprentices work every day for two years.

_____ b. Tigers are majestic creatures.

_____ c. Tiger trainers should earn less money than they do.

2. From the article, you can predict that if the tiger had not been distracted during Roy Horn's fateful show,

☐ a. the crowd would have been bored.

☐ b. the show would have gone on as usual.

☐ c. the tiger would have attacked Horn anyway.

3. Choose from the letters below to correctly complete the following statement. Write the letters on the lines.

In the article, _____ and _____ are different because they use different tiger training techniques.

a. Chris Heiden

b. Roy Horn

c. Tabayara Maluenda

4. Choose from the letters below to correctly complete the following statement. Write the letters on the lines.

According to the article, _____ caused the 380-pound white tiger to _____, and the effect was _____.

a. sink its teeth into Roy's neck

b. Roy lost massive amounts of blood

c. Roy Horn's falling backward

5. What did you have to do to answer question 3?

☐ a. find a cause (why something happened)

☐ b. find an opinion (what someone thinks about something)

☐ c. find a contrast (how things are different)

_____ Number of correct answers

Record your personal assessment of your work on the Critical Thinking Chart on page 58.

Personal Response

A question I would like answered by Roy Horn is

_____

_____

_____

_____

Self-Assessment

One good question about this article that was not asked would be

_____

_____

_____

_____

and the answer is

_____

_____

_____

_____

Compare and Contrast

Think about the articles you have read in Unit One. Choose three articles that describe jobs you would like to have someday. Write the titles of the articles that tell about them in the first column of the chart below. Use information you learned from the articles to fill in the empty boxes in the chart.

Title	What skills or personal qualities does this job require?	What are the risks of the job?	How would independent thinking benefit a person in this job?

A maverick I would most like to learn from is _____. I chose this person because _____

_____

Words-per-Minute Table

Unit One

Directions If you were timed while reading an article, refer to the Reading Time you recorded in the box at the end of the article. Use this words-per-minute table to determine your reading speed for that article. Then plot your reading speed on the graph on page 56.

Lesson	Sample	1	2	3	4	5	
No. of Words	1112	1211	1015	1095	1116	1167	
1:30	741	807	677	730	744	778	**90**
1:40	667	727	609	657	670	700	**100**
1:50	607	661	554	597	609	637	**110**
2:00	556	606	508	548	558	584	**120**
2:10	513	559	468	505	515	539	**130**
2:20	477	519	435	469	478	500	**140**
2:30	445	484	406	438	446	467	**150**
2:40	417	454	381	411	419	438	**160**
2:50	392	427	358	386	394	412	**170**
3:00	371	404	338	365	372	389	**180**
3:10	351	382	321	346	352	369	**190**
3:20	334	363	305	329	335	350	**200**
3:30	318	346	290	313	319	333	**210**
3:40	303	330	277	299	304	318	**220**
3:50	290	316	265	286	291	304	**230**
4:00	278	303	254	274	279	292	**240**
4:10	267	291	244	263	268	280	**250**
4:20	257	279	234	253	258	269	**260**
4:30	247	269	226	243	248	259	**270**
4:40	238	260	218	235	239	250	**280**
4:50	230	251	210	227	231	241	**290**
5:00	222	242	203	219	223	233	**300**
5:10	215	234	196	212	216	226	**310**
5:20	209	227	190	205	209	219	**320**
5:30	202	220	185	199	203	212	**330**
5:40	196	214	179	193	197	206	**340**
5:50	191	208	174	188	191	200	**350**
6:00	185	202	169	183	186	195	**360**
6:10	180	196	165	178	181	189	**370**
6:20	176	191	160	173	176	184	**380**
6:30	171	186	156	168	172	180	**390**
6:40	167	182	152	164	167	175	**400**
6:50	163	177	149	160	163	171	**410**
7:00	159	173	145	156	159	167	**420**
7:10	155	169	142	153	156	163	**430**
7:20	152	165	138	149	152	159	**440**
7:30	148	161	135	146	149	156	**450**
7:40	145	158	132	143	146	152	**460**
7:50	142	155	130	140	142	149	**470**
8:00	139	151	127	137	140	146	**480**

Minutes and Seconds

Seconds

Plotting Your Progress: Reading Speed

Unit One

Directions If you were timed while reading an article, write your words-per-minute rate for that article in the box under the number of the lesson. Then plot your reading speed on the graph by putting a small X on the line directly above the number of the lesson, across from the number of words per minute you read. As you mark your speed for each lesson, graph your progress by drawing a line to connect the Xs.

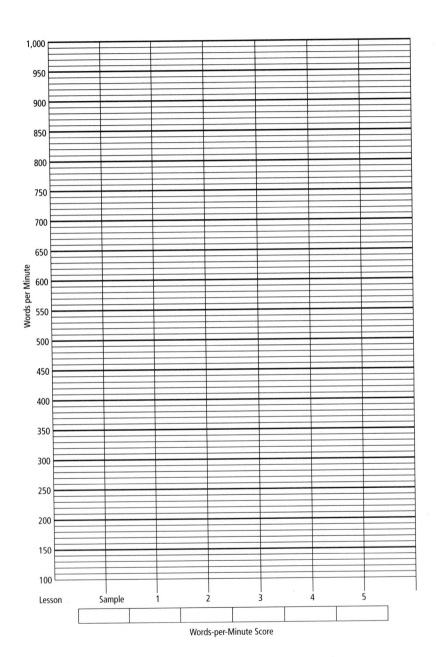

Words per Minute

Lesson   Sample   1   2   3   4   5

Words-per-Minute Score

Plotting Your Progress: Reading Comprehension

Unit One

Directions Write your Reading Comprehension score for each lesson in the box under the number of the lesson. Then plot your score on the graph by putting a small X on the line directly above the number of the lesson and across from the score you earned. As you mark your score for each lesson, graph your progress by drawing a line to connect the Xs.

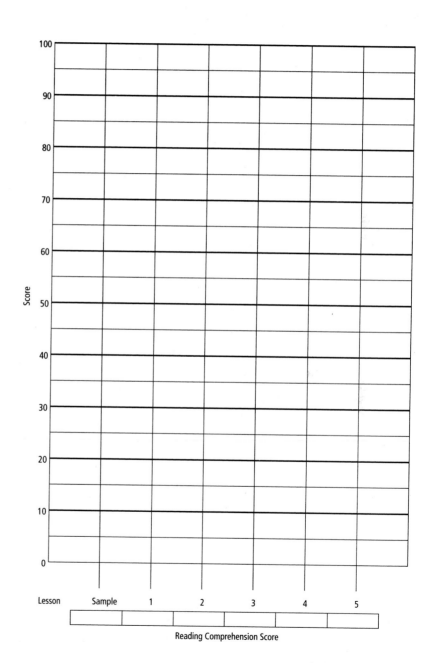

Score

Lesson   Sample   1   2   3   4   5

Reading Comprehension Score

Plotting Your Progress: Critical Thinking

Unit One

Directions Work with your teacher to evaluate your responses to the Critical Thinking questions for each lesson. Then fill in the appropriate spaces in the chart below. For each lesson and each type of Critical Thinking question, do the following: Mark a minus sign (–) in the box to indicate areas in which you feel you could improve. Mark a plus sign (+) to indicate areas in which you feel you did well. Mark a minus-slash-plus sign (–/+) to indicate areas in which you had mixed success. Then write any comments you have about your performance, including ideas for improvement.

Lesson	Author's Approach	Summarizing and Paraphrasing	Critical Thinking
Sample			
1			
2			
3			
4			
5			

Unit Two

Bomb Squad

No False Moves

A bomb disposal officer from Iraqi security forces defuses a bomb found in a cemetery in the village of Qara Tappah in Iraq.

You know it's a tough job when you're walking one way and everyone else is running in the opposite direction. But that's life for members of the bomb squad, who call the approach toward a live bomb "the long walk" regardless of the actual distance. Their primary job is to find and disarm a bomb before it can do damage to anyone or anything in the area. Their second job is to not die doing it. These days, bomb squads do most of their work with booby traps called IEDs (improvised explosive devices). These devices have killed more American soldiers in Iraq and Afghanistan than any other weapon. Bomb squads are deployed by some police departments in the United States on occasion, but it is in the Iraqi and Afghanistan war zones that bomb squad members are on constant alert.

2   A bomb squad has a rhythm similar to a fire department, with its quiet lulls suddenly turning into wild action. In Iraq and Afghanistan, those restful lulls can be few and far between. Insurgents or terrorists plant thousands of IEDs every year along roads and paths where people travel. A bomb squad member stationed in Baghdad, the capital of Iraq, has been described as similar to a firefighter in a city full of arsonists. One intersection of two highways has been planted with so many IEDs that it has been nicknamed "Death X."

3   With all the carnage these hidden bombs cause to soldiers and civilians, defusing them is one of the most important jobs in a war zone. It is also one of the most dangerous. Bomb squad Sergeant Jeffrey McClean describes it this way. "We are the emergency response unit, the 'Bomb Squad' whose mission is to render IEDs inoperable. And yes, it's a dangerous duty, but it's a job we're proud to perform."

4   The key word in IEDs is *improvised*. These bombs are not mass produced in a munitions factory. If they were, they would not be nearly so dangerous, because they could all be disarmed in the same way. Because IEDs are made by individuals with whatever materials that happen to be available, each one is unique. The triggering mechanism, for example, might be something low-tech like a garage door opener, doorbell, or car alarm. A more advanced trigger might be made from a cell phone or the remote control from a toy car. One terrorist might use dynamite and a timer taken from an old washing machine. Another terrorist might use fertilizer as the explosive and hook it up to a battery and a cordless telephone.

5   To make matters even more difficult, insurgents share their tactics on the Internet. So the constant worry facing a bomb squad is that today's IED will be different from yesterday's IED. It's a cat-and-mouse game,

A remote control robot moves a pressure plate taken from an IED that was discovered during a route-clearance mission near Khakriz, Afghanistan.

with each side trying to stay one step ahead of the other. Colonel Jeffrey Jarkowsky, leader of a bomb squad unit in Afghanistan, was asked how he felt after five Americans were killed in less than a week by IEDs. "We take each one of these personally," he replied. "Every time we see one of these casualties, we look at what happened." Bomb squad members try to see what the enemy did so that they can prevent a similar incident from happening again.

6　An IED can be hidden anywhere. Terrorists might put one in a tunnel or an old soda bottle or under a mound of trash. They might tuck one inside the rim of a discarded tire or hide it in the crack of a wall. They have even planted explosives inside animal carcasses along the highway. The list of places to hide an IED is virtually endless. Bomb squad members must constantly be on the lookout for anything— anything at all—that looks even a bit suspicious or out of the ordinary.

7　Bomb squad members know that insurgents will sometimes plant a second or third bomb close to the first one. This so-called "daisy chain" cluster is used to produce a particularly massive explosion. So defusing one bomb doesn't always mean that you are in the clear. Then, too, there is the danger of being shot. Imagine you've found an IED on the median strip of a highway. As you are working to defuse it, you have to wonder if there is a sniper lurking on a rooftop just waiting to pick you off. Major Chris Hunter, a British bomb disposal specialist, says "There's a tremendous sense of vulnerability . . . you're considering where they may have placed a second device and whether a sniper has you in his cross-hairs."

8　The military is constantly working to reduce the dangers faced by its bomb squads. The primary focus has been on finding ways to locate and disarm IEDs from as far away as possible. In the early days of the war, bomb squad members donned protective suits and walked right up to the bomb to disarm it. Sergeant Willard Peterson calls this tactic "effective but dangerous." He says, "I lost a lot of friends like that." He describes one friend who went looking for bombs near a wall loaded with anti-American graffiti. The soldier found a bomb, but before he could defuse it, a terrorist ignited it, blowing up both the wall and Peterson's friend.

9　More recently, the army has begun to rely on robots to probe anything that looks suspicious. These three-foot-high devices move on treads. They have a crab-like arm to investigate potential bombs and can be directed with a joystick from a safe distance. The robots are able to cut wires to a bomb or plant their own explosives to blow up the IED. Even more advanced is a 27-foot-long vehicle known as the "Buffalo." It has a long mechanical arm with a nine-pronged claw that can probe for IEDs.

10　Even with the most advanced equipment, however, the human element is still needed. There was one time in Afghanistan, for example, when a bomb got stuck between the prongs of the Buffalo's claw. No amount of shaking the arm from inside the vehicle would free it. Finally, three soldiers leapt out of the vehicle, risking their lives to untangle the IED from the claw by hand. After struggling desperately for 15 minutes, they finally got it loose. They then managed to transport the bomb to a safe location and blow it up without causing any harm. The blast was so big that it would have destroyed an armored truck and killed all of its crew. As one bomb squad member later said, "It makes me feel a whole lot better that we found it, instead of it finding us." It's those sorts of victories that keep bomb squad members motivated. But it takes a special person to face such dangers day after day after day. ✳

If you have been timed while reading this article, enter your reading time below. Then turn to the Words-per-Minute Table on page 101 and look up your reading speed (words per minute). Enter your reading speed on the graph on page 102.

Reading Time: Lesson 6

_____ : _____
Minutes   *Seconds*

A Finding the Main Idea

One statement below expresses the main idea of the article. One statement is too general, or too broad. The other statement explains only part of the article; it is too narrow. Label the statements using the following key:

M—Main Idea   **B—Too Broad**   **N—Too Narrow**

_____ 1. Members of bomb squads have a dangerous duty to perform.

_____ 2. A bomb squad has a rhythm similar to a fire department.

_____ 3. Members of bomb squads find and disarm bombs before the bombs can damage anyone or anything in the area.

_____ Score 15 points for a correct M answer.

_____ Score 5 points for each correct B or N answer.

_____ **Total Score**: Finding the Main Idea

B Recalling Facts

How well do you remember the facts in the article? Put an X in the box next to the answer that correctly completes each statement about the article.

1. The name that members of bomb squads have given to the walk toward a suspected bomb is
   - ☐ a. "the walk of fear."
   - ☐ b. "the walk of death."
   - ☐ c. "the long walk."

2. The initials IED stand for
   - ☐ a. improved exploding device.
   - ☐ b. improvised explosive device.
   - ☐ c. invented exploding device.

3. Baghdad is the capital of
   - ☐ a. Iran.
   - ☐ b. Iraq.
   - ☐ c. Afghanistan.

4. A "daisy chain" cluster of bombs refers to
   - ☐ a. a set of bombs planted one mile apart each.
   - ☐ b. a group of bombs hidden in a field.
   - ☐ c. a set of two or three bombs planted close together.

5. In this article, "Buffalo" is the name given to
   - ☐ a. a 27-foot-long vehicle with a nine-pronged claw.
   - ☐ b. a small robot.
   - ☐ c. a bomb made with a unique triggering mechanism.

Score 5 points for each correct answer.

_____ **Total Score**: Recalling Facts

C Making Inferences

When you combine your own experiences and information from a text to draw a conclusion that is not directly stated in that text, you are making an inference. Below are five statements that may or may not be inferences based on information in the article. Label the statements using the following key:

C—Correct Inference   **F—Faulty Inference**

_____ 1. Terrorists in the war zones of Iraq and Afghanistan were the first to make IEDs.

_____ 2. Many IEDs are small in size.

_____ 3. American soldiers in Iraq and Afghanistan appreciate and respect bomb squad members.

_____ 4. Because no one can stand the tension of such a dangerous job for very long, bomb squad members get frequent days off duty.

_____ 5. Bomb squad members undergo a great deal of training before they face their first live bomb.

Score 5 points for each correct answer.

_____ **Total Score**: Making Inferences

D Using Words Precisely

Each numbered sentence below contains an underlined word or phrase from the article. Following the sentence are three definitions. One definition is closest to the meaning of the underlined word. One definition is opposite or nearly opposite. Label those two definitions using the following key. Do not label the remaining definition.

C—Closest   **O—Opposite or Nearly Opposite**

1. With all the <u>carnage</u> these hidden bombs cause to soldiers and civilians, defusing them is one of the most important jobs in a war zone.

_____ a. loud noise

_____ b. lasting peace

_____ c. killing in great numbers

2. "We are the emergency response unit, the 'Bomb Squad' whose mission is to render IEDs <u>inoperable</u>."

_____ a. running smoothly

_____ b. not able to work; broken

_____ c. dangerous

3. The list of places to hide an IED is <u>virtually</u> endless.

_____ a. almost, but not in actual fact

_____ b. far from being

_____ c. unfortunately

4. When you are defusing a bomb in a war zone, there is a tremendous sense of <u>vulnerability</u>.

_____ a. needing to hurry

_____ b. feeling safe

_____ c. being open to harm

5. It's those sorts of victories that keep bomb squad members <u>motivated</u>.

_____ a. discouraged

_____ b. relieved

_____ c. eager to act

_____ Score 3 points for each correct C answer.

_____ Score 2 points for each correct O answer.

_____ **Total Score**: Using Words Precisely

Enter the four total scores in the spaces below, and add them together to find your Reading Comprehension Score. Then record your score on the graph on page 103.

Score	Question Type	Lesson 6
_____	Finding the Main Idea	
_____	Recalling Facts	
_____	Making Inferences	
_____	Using Words Precisely	
_____	**Reading Comprehension Score**	

Author's Approach

Put an X in the box next to the correct answer.

1. What is the author's purpose in writing this article?

☐ a. to encourage the reader to learn more about the wars in Iraq and Afghanistan

☐ b. to inform the reader about the work of military bomb squads

☐ c. to describe what happens to soldiers in a war zone

2. From the statements below, choose the one [or ones] that you believe the author would agree with.

☐ a. The robots used by bomb squads have saved lives.

☐ b. The robots used by bomb squads have proven to be unreliable.

☐ c. The robots used by bomb squads have made defusing bombs safer.

3. Choose the statement below from the last paragraph that best describes the author's opinion of military bomb squads.

☐ a. "Even with the most advanced equipment, however, the human element is still needed."

☐ b. "Finally, three soldiers leapt out of the vehicle, risking their lives to untangle the IED from the claw by hand."

☐ c. "But it takes a special person to face the dangers of defusing bombs day after day after day."

4. Which of the following statements from the article best describes the way bomb squad members feel about their work?

☐ a. "A bomb squad has a rhythm similar to a fire department."

☐ b. "We take each American soldier's death personally."

☐ c. "It's a dangerous duty, but it's a job we're proud to perform."

_____ Number of correct answers

Record your personal assessment of your work on the Critical Thinking Chart on page 104.

CRITICAL THINKING

Summarizing and Paraphrasing

Follow the directions provided for question 1. Put an X in the box next to the correct answer for the other questions.

1. Reread paragraph 7 in the article. Below, write a summary of the paragraph in no more than 25 words.

   _____

   _____

   _____

   _____

2. Below are summaries of the article. Choose the summary that says all the most important things about the article but in the fewest words.

   ☐ a. Military bomb squads find and disarm bombs. Many work in war zones, defusing IEDs. Defusing bombs is very dangerous, even with the use of advanced equipment.

   ☐ b. Bomb squad members defuse bombs and many work in the war zones of Iraq and Afghanistan.

   ☐ c. The job of bomb squads is very dangerous because they work mainly with IEDs, each of which is unique.

3. Choose the sentence that correctly restates the following sentence from the article: "Even with the most advanced equipment, however, the human element is still needed."

   ☐ a. Humans can do jobs better than even the most advanced equipment.

   ☐ b. Despite having the best equipment, a bomb squad still needs the skills of a human being.

   ☐ c. Humans still need the best equipment available.

   _____ Number of correct answers

   Record your personal assessment of your work on the Critical Thinking Chart on page 104.

Critical Thinking

Put an X next to the correct answer for questions 1, 4, and 5. Follow the directions provided for the other questions.

1. From what the article told about the robots and other equipment used by bomb squads, you can predict that

   ☐ a. the Army will continue to develop them to reduce the danger to bomb squad members.

   ☐ b. the Army will stop their use because they are not as dependable as people.

   ☐ c. they will replace bomb squads so people will not have to risk their lives to defuse bombs.

2. Choose from the letters below to correctly complete the following statement. Write the letters on the lines.

   In the article _____ and _____ are alike because they both have slow periods followed by incredibly busy times.

   a. bomb squads

   b. fire departments

   c. soldiers

3. Reread the last paragraph. Then choose from the letters below to correctly complete the following statement. Write the letters on the lines.

   According to the last paragraph, _____ because _____.

   a. three soldiers untangled a bomb by hand

   b. an armored truck was blown up

   c. an IED was stuck in a Buffalo's claws

CRITICAL THINKING

4. Of the following theme categories, which would this story fit into?

☐ a. Robotics

☐ b. Modern Warfare

☐ c. Journeys

5. From the information in paragraph 2, you can conclude that

☐ a. there are more bomb squads in the capital of Iraq than anywhere else in the country.

☐ b. terrorists kill civilians as well as soldiers.

☐ c. terrorists have planted more bombs in Iraq than in Afghanistan.

_____ Number of correct answers

Record your personal assessment of your work on the Critical Thinking Chart on page 104.

Personal Response

If you could ask the author of the article one question, what would it be?

_____

_____

_____

_____

Self-Assessment

I was confused about question _____ in the _____ section because

_____

_____

_____

_____

_____

_____

_____

_____

Sherpas
Helpers in High Altitudes

The icy, high-altitude slopes of Mount Everest on the Nepal-Tibet border were considered off-limits to foreign mountain climbers until Sherpas were employed to assist them.

It is not a career that many people would find appealing. The Help Wanted ad would read something like this: *Assistant needed for expeditions to the most desolate locations on Earth. Must be willing to brave sub-zero temperatures, hurricane-force winds, and extreme heights, all while carrying 80 pounds of food and equipment. Pay is minimal; risks include frostbite, altitude sickness, snow blindness, hypothermia, and death.* Given that job description, it is surprising that anyone would choose to be a Sherpa guide. What may be even more astonishing is that Sherpa guides are so good at what they do.

2   "Sherpa" is actually not a job title; it is the name for an ethnic group that moved into the Himalayan Mountains from eastern Tibet more than 500 years ago. The word *Sherpa* literally means "people from the east." Ever since westerners began climbing in the region in the 1920s, however, mountaineers have relied on Sherpas for help, and so, over time, the term has become synonymous with the courageous souls who guide explorers to the tops of such peaks as K2, Annapurna, and Mount Everest.

3   In a typical modern expedition, Sherpas do most of the heavy lifting—quite literally. They carry the equipment, food, and oxygen tanks that climbers need to get to the top of the world's highest mountains. Sherpas help prepare the path for an ascent, clearing away ice and anchoring the ropes that will serve as lifelines along the frozen cliffs. In addition, they do most of the cooking and other customary duties around each base camp. In short, they are vital to high-altitude expeditions. And that's true even when things go well.

4   It's when things go wrong that Sherpas really prove indispensable. Again and again Sherpas have stepped in to perform heroic tasks in an attempt to rescue a climber in trouble. In 2010 Spanish climber Tolo Calafat was 24,000 feet up on Annapurna when his brain began swelling due to the thin atmosphere. The Sherpa assisting him, Sonam, did not leave his side even as weather conditions deteriorated and darkness settled over the mountain. All night long, Sonam stayed with Tolo, trying to get the unresponsive climber to move.

The next morning, Sonam finally left Tolo and made his way through swirling snow to the base camp. When he arrived, he found all the climbers there exhausted from their previous day's summit. Yet one man—a fellow Sherpa named Dawa—agreed to go back up the mountain in a last-ditch effort to save Tolo. "The truth is that he did not hesitate," climber Carlos Pauner later reported. "Taking oxygen, food, medicines, and a sleeping bag, he took off to meet Tolo." Dawa searched desperately for 11 hours, but heavy snow had erased every trace of the Spanish climber. Dawa himself was lucky to make it back to camp alive.

5   In 2008 Pemba Gyalje Sherpa performed a series of heroic actions in the wake of an

Sherpas are spiritually connected to Mount Everest while also benefiting from Westerners' passion for mountain climbing.

avalanche that struck near the top of K2. At the time, 17 climbers, including Pemba, were high up in the "death zone," the label given to terrain above 26,000 feet. They had summited and were just beginning their descent, heading into a particularly treacherous stretch called the Bottleneck. Suddenly, a massive block of ice gave way and careened down the mountain, carrying with it most of the ropes that had been anchored onto the slope. The avalanche killed one climber outright and swept away several others. Those who remained were trapped at 27,000 feet with no fixed ropes to continue their descent. Desperate, Pemba Gyalje Sherpa began climbing down the steep, icy Bottleneck without ropes. Long into the night he picked his way down, arriving at the safety of the 25,000-foot Base Camp 4 at 1 a.m.

6   At daybreak, Pemba gathered his energy and headed back up the mountain with rescue ropes and oxygen tanks. Halfway up the Bottleneck, he found Italian climber Marco Confortola lying unconscious in the snow. Pemba revived him with oxygen, saving him from certain death. He then began helping the weakened climber toward the base of the Bottleneck. At that point, another avalanche hit. "I was falling," Marco later recalled. "The avalanche would have taken me away. But Pemba grabbed me from behind." For the second time that morning, Pemba Gyalje Sherpa had saved Marco's life.

7   As it turned out, Pemba's ordeal was far from over. By the time he got Marco to safety, he was completely exhausted. Yet a few hours later he headed out yet again, this time in search of a Dutch mountaineer who was alive but who had become disoriented after the avalanche. The man had wandered to a remote portion of the mountain, far from the established climbing route. It took Pemba many hours and two separate attempts, but he finally found the Dutch man and brought him back to camp alive.

8   How is it that Sherpas such as Sonam, Dawa, and Pemba Gyalje have such remarkable stamina when so many climbers have collapsed in exhaustion? Part of the answer lies in their lifestyle. "Many Sherpas are born and raised at heights of more than 13,000 feet," explains one Sherpa. Another reports that most of them spend their childhood grazing their cattle or yaks at high altitudes, routinely climbing to heights between 18,000 and 19,000 feet without jackets or mountaineering gear. In other words, Sherpas are used to the conditions that greet them on the world's tallest mountains. Genes may also play a role, since studies have shown that Sherpas use less energy when climbing and can stay healthy with less oxygen than other people.

9   There is an economic incentive as well. Sherpas are not wealthy people. They become high-altitude guides because it pays better than growing barley or tending yaks. While few westerners would risk their lives for a couple thousand dollars a year, that sum is enough to attract an estimated 15,000 Sherpas to the profession. And since a good reputation means they are more likely to get hired by the top-paying expeditions, Sherpas do everything they can to prove their worth.

10   Beyond that, however, most Sherpa guides have proven themselves to be amazingly selfless and courageous. They have repeatedly risked their lives to help those in need. Recalling Dawa Sherpa's attempts to find Tolo Calafat, Carlos Pauner says, "Dawa made an extraordinary sacrifice, not for money, not for glory, not for fame. He did it just because he understood that he was the only one that could do it." Such efforts have sometimes cost Sherpas their lives. More than 50 have died on Mount Everest alone. Yet every year Sherpa guides return to the highest mountains on Earth and do what they can to help others reach the summits. ✳

If you have been timed while reading this article, enter your reading time below. Then turn to the Words-per-Minute Table on page 101 and look up your reading speed (words per minute). Enter your reading speed on the graph on page 102.

Reading Time: Lesson 7

_____ : _____

Minutes   *Seconds*

A Finding the Main Idea

One statement below expresses the main idea of the article. One statement is too general, or too broad. The other statement explains only part of the article; it is too narrow. Label the statements using the following key:

M—Main Idea   **B—Too Broad**   **N—Too Narrow**

_____ 1. Sherpa guides often risk their lives to rescue injured or trapped climbers.

_____ 2. Sherpas are brave, strong people who are invaluable to Himalayan mountain climbers.

_____ 3. Sherpas are very good at guiding mountain climbers.

_____ Score 15 points for a correct M answer.

_____ Score 5 points for each correct B or N answer.

_____ **Total Score**: Finding the Main Idea

B Recalling Facts

How well do you remember the facts in the article? Put an X in the box next to the answer that correctly completes each statement about the article.

1. *Sherpa* literally means
   - ☐ a. "mountain climber guides."
   - ☐ b. "people of the Himalayan Mountains."
   - ☐ c. "people from the east."

2. One of the jobs of a Sherpa is
   - ☐ a. buying supplies needed for an expedition.
   - ☐ b. carrying supplies needed for an expedition.
   - ☐ c. providing medical assistance on an expedition.

3. The Sherpa named Dawa
   - ☐ a. rescued the climber Tolo Calafat despite heavy snow.
   - ☐ b. searched for Tolo Calafat but could not find him.
   - ☐ c. was too exhausted to join in the search for Tolo.

4. The Italian climber Marco Confortola
   - ☐ a. climbed down the icy Bottleneck without ropes.
   - ☐ b. was killed by an avalanche.
   - ☐ c. was rescued by Pemba Gyalje Sherpa.

5. For the dangerous work they do, Sherpas are paid
   - ☐ a. a few thousand dollars a year.
   - ☐ b. an estimated $15,000 a year.
   - ☐ c. in barley, yaks, and cattle.

Score 5 points for each correct answer.

_____ **Total Score**: Recalling Facts

C Making Inferences

When you combine your own experiences and information from a text to draw a conclusion that is not directly stated in that text, you are making an inference. Below are five statements that may or may not be inferences based on information in the article. Label the statements using the following key:

C—Correct Inference   **F—Faulty Inference**

_____ 1. People from many parts of the world come to climb the highest peaks of the Himalayan Mountains.

_____ 2. Sherpas spend their childhoods at high altitudes to prepare themselves to become mountain climber guides.

_____ 3. Western climbers are not capable of doing the jobs that Sherpas do.

_____ 4. Mountain climbing is a very exhausting activity.

_____ 5. Sherpas do not like mountain climbing but lead expeditions for the money.

Score 5 points for each correct answer.

_____ **Total Score:** Making Inferences

D Using Words Precisely

Each numbered sentence below contains an underlined word or phrase from the article. Following the sentence are three definitions. One definition is closest to the meaning of the underlined word. One definition is opposite or nearly opposite. Label those two definitions using the following key. Do not label the remaining definition.

C—Closest   **O—Opposite or Nearly Opposite**

1. The term *Sherpas* has become <u>synonymous</u> with the courageous souls who guide explorers to the tops of peaks.

_____ a. dangerous

_____ b. different

_____ c. the same; identical

2. Sherpas do most of the cooking and other <u>customary</u> duties around each base camp.

_____ a. routine

_____ b. difficult

_____ c. unusual

3. It's when things go wrong that Sherpas really prove <u>indispensable</u>.

_____ a. very important

_____ b. unnecessary

_____ c. brave

4. How is it that Sherpas have such remarkable <u>stamina</u> when so many climbers have collapsed in exhaustion?

_____ a. tendency toward laziness

_____ b. gifts for leadership

_____ c. ability to endure

5. There is an economic <u>incentive</u> for Sherpas to become mountain guides as well.

_____ a. trend

_____ b. motivation

_____ c. obstacle

_____ Score 3 points for each correct C answer.

_____ Score 2 points for each correct O answer.

_____ **Total Score:** Using Words Precisely

Enter the four total scores in the spaces below, and add them together to find your Reading Comprehension Score. Then record your score on the graph on page 103.

Score	Question Type	Lesson 7
_____	Finding the Main Idea	
_____	Recalling Facts	
_____	Making Inferences	
_____	Using Words Precisely	
_____	**Reading Comprehension Score**	

Author's Approach

Put an X in the box next to the correct answer.

1. What is the author's purpose in writing this article?
☐ a. to encourage the reader to take up mountain climbing
☐ b. to inform the reader about the role Sherpas play in mountain climbing expeditions
☐ c. to describe what mountain climbers do

2. From the statements below, choose the one [or ones] that you believe the author would agree with.
☐ a. Anyone would be foolish to attempt mountain climbing in the Himalayas without a Sherpa guide.
☐ b. Sherpas resent the people they help to climb the Himalayan Mountains.
☐ c. In the future, mountain climbers will avoid the Himalayas because they are so dangerous.

3. The author tells this story mainly by
☐ a. describing the daily life of the Sherpas.
☐ b. listing facts about mountain climbing.
☐ c. giving examples of Sherpa bravery.

4. Judging by statements from the article, you can conclude that the author wants the reader to think that
☐ a. the Sherpas are a people we should admire.
☐ b. the Sherpas are a people we should pity.
☐ c. the Sherpas are greedy.

_____ Number of correct answers

Record your personal assessment of your work on the Critical Thinking Chart on page 104.

CRITICAL THINKING

Summarizing and Paraphrasing

Follow the directions provided for question 1. Put an X in the box next to the correct answer for the other questions.

1. Complete the following one-sentence summary of the article using the lettered phrases from the phrase bank below. Write the letters on the lines.

> **Phrase Bank:**
> a. stories of Sherpa courage and strength
> b. a description of the job of Sherpa guide
> c. praise for the selflessness of the Sherpa guides

The article "Sherpas: Helpers in High Altitudes" begins with _____, goes on to describe _____, and ends with _____.

2. Read the statement from the article below. Then read the paraphrase of that statement. Choose the reason that best tells why the paraphrase does not say the same thing as the statement.

   Statement: Yet every year Sherpa guides return to the highest mountains on Earth and do what they can to help others reach the summits.

   Paraphrase: Year after year, Sherpas act as guides for other people who are part of mountain-climbing expeditions.

   ☐ a.   Paraphrase says too much.

   ☐ b.   Paraphrase doesn't say enough.

   ☐ c.   Paraphrase doesn't agree with the statement.

3. Choose the sentence that correctly restates the following sentence from the article: "They had summited and were just beginning their descent, heading into a particularly treacherous stretch called the Bottleneck."

   ☐ a.   They had reached the mountain peak and were coming down, entering a dangerous area called the Bottleneck.

   ☐ b.   They had given up and were climbing down, trying to avoid the slippery region called the Bottleneck.

   ☐ c.   They were tired and decided to climb down to their base camp in the Bottleneck.

> _____ Number of correct answers
>
> Record your personal assessment of your work on the Critical Thinking Chart on page 104.

Critical Thinking

Follow the directions provided for questions 2 and 5. Put an X next to the correct answer for the other questions.

1. Which of the following statements from the article is an opinion rather than a fact?

   ☐ a.   In a typical modern expedition, Sherpas do most of the heavy lifting—quite literally.

   ☐ b.   It is not a career that many people would find appealing.

   ☐ c.   The avalanche killed one climber and swept away several others.

2. Choose from the letters below to correctly complete the following statement. Write the letters on the lines.

   On the positive side, _____, but on the negative side _____.

   a.   guiding a mountain climbing expedition can be very risky

   b.   being a Sherpa guide pays better than farming or raising yaks

   c.   Sherpa guides have proven themselves to be amazingly brave

CRITICAL THINKING

3. What was the effect of the avalanche that struck near the top of K2 in 2008?

☐ a. Seventeen climbers were high up in the "death zone."

☐ b. The climbers' base camp was at a height of 25,000 feet.

☐ c. Several climbers were trapped at 27,000 feet.

4. Judging by events in the article, you can conclude that

☐ a. Sherpas would prefer to raise cattle than guide mountain climbers.

☐ b. mountain climbing is both difficult and dangerous.

☐ c. Pemba Gyalje Sherpa will never guide another mountain climbing expedition.

5. In which paragraph did you find your information or details to answer question 3?

_____

_____ Number of correct answers

Record your personal assessment of your work on the Critical Thinking Chart on page 104.

Personal Response

A question I would like answered by the Sherpa named Dawa is

_____

_____

_____

_____

Self-Assessment

I can't really understand how

_____

_____

_____

_____

_____

_____

_____

_____

_____

_____

_____

CRITICAL THINKING

Bull Riders

Ride or Run!

Bull riders must stay on the bull for eight whole seconds, which may seem like a very long time to some riders.

In the abstract, it sounds easy enough to do. All you have to do is take a nice comfortable seat, grab hold of a flat, braided rope with one hand, and stay seated for eight seconds. Ready? Start counting: one thousand one, one thousand two, one thousand three. Believe it or not, there's a good chance that before you reach "one thousand eight," you will find yourself sprawled face-down in the dirt or running for your life. That is because the seat you took was on the back of an angry, not-to-be-messed-with 2,000-pound bucking bull, whose entire purpose was to dump you off his back and then maybe stomp on your head.

2   There is a good reason why rodeo bull riding is often called "the most dangerous eight seconds in sports." Just ask bull rider Mike Lee. In 2003 he was competing at the Professional Rodeo Cowboys Association rodeo in Fort Smith, Arkansas. Lee took his seat atop a bull named Chili in a claustrophobic gated steel chute barely big enough to hold bull and rider. When the gate sprang open, Chili began bucking furiously. After just six seconds, the bull threw Lee in a way that caused the rider's skull to collide with Chili's skull. Lee doesn't remember anything after that. "There was blood gushing from the right side of my skull, but I only remember waking up in the hospital."

3   It took Lee four months to recuperate sufficiently from brain surgery to ride again. Asked why he continued to risk life and limb to ride bulls, Mike Lee responded,

"I love it. It's hard to imagine doing anything else for a living. Head injury or not, this is the greatest sport alive—and I live for those eight seconds."

4   Although Mike Lee lived to ride another day, many others have not been so fortunate. On average, one or two bull riders die every year. In 2005, for example, Daniel Dopps died from the injuries he suffered when the bull he was riding flipped and fell on top of him. Earlier that year, Anthony Covington died when he hit his head against the bull's

head and then had his chest crushed by the bull's hooves. Even when a rider completes his eight-second ride, danger still lurks. In 2007 Joshua "Cody" Brunner was stepped on and killed by a bull right after he dismounted. In all of these cases, the explanation is the same: "It was just a freak accident." No one in the industry seems to question the sanity of riding on the back of an agitated bull.

5   People who know nothing about the rodeo might be surprised to learn that

The rodeo clown (in suspenders, right) must distract the angry bull away from the rider that has been thrown off.

women and young children also ride. Although junior competitors ride smaller bulls, that certainly does not eliminate the risks inherent in the sport. In 2009 a 12-year-old boy, who had already been riding for six years, was riding in the Little Britches Rodeo in Colorado when a 1,200-pound bull tossed him and then stepped on his chest. Despite the fact that the boy was wearing a helmet and a protective vest, the impact of the bull's hoof ruptured his heart and killed him. As usual, rodeo lovers claimed that it was just a "freak accident."

6　　Women have been features at rodeos since the 1880s, when sharpshooter Annie Oakley starred in Wild West shows. Today, women ride bucking bulls just like the men do. The animals they ride are just as big and just as angry as those ridden by men. Although women are allowed to use two hands (men must use just one hand), none of them do. It is simply part of the unwritten Wild West code. Also, like the men, women who ride claim that bull riding is just part of who they are. Tammy Kelly, a five-time world champion, once remarked, "Most women are not raised to do any kind of rough sport, especially riding bulls, but I believe this is what I was raised to be."

7　　Casual observers might wonder why rodeo bulls go so berserk as soon as the gate springs open. Do these bulls have a personal grudge against their riders? The truth is that bulls buck and spin so frantically not because of the riders but because of the flank rope, or strap, tied tightly around the bull's belly at its hips. As one rider explained, "They are actually trying to kick the flank rope off. If we didn't tie the flank rope on, they'd just shoot out of the chute and run in a straight line."

8　　The use of this flank strap has stirred up bitter controversy, especially with animal rights groups such as PETA (People for the Ethical Treatment of Animals). Critics argue that the flank strap amounts to nothing less than animal torture. In addition to the extreme discomfort the strap causes, the bull's enraged bucking sometimes causes unintended but severe injury to the animal. There is a second reason why the bull charges out of the chute angry at the world. To ensure an entertaining ride, the bull is sometimes prodded with a powerful electric jolt just before the chute opens. So while rodeo fans may be thrilled by the daring and agility of the bull riders, it is clearly no picnic for the bull.

9　　In many ways, bull riding is caught between two contradictory worlds. On the one hand, the sport is growing in popularity as it reaches a broader, more urban audience through television and digital media. There is an undeniable thirst in 21st century sports fans for more violence and more danger. Just look at the explosive growth of "extreme sports." On the other hand, people are now more sensitive to animal cruelty. By 2010 the once-popular sport of dog racing, now often viewed as cruel to the dogs, had been voted illegal in all but a few states.

10　　Despite its critics, bull riding remains a popular form of entertainment, particularly in the American West. Bull riders continue to risk their lives because of the challenge and the money. The most successful and skillful riders earn hundreds of thousands of dollars per year. But they also have to be lucky to avoid that "freak" accident. Every time the chute opens, they know that the next eight seconds could be their last. ✳

If you have been timed while reading this article, enter your reading time below. Then turn to the Words-per-Minute Table on page 101 and look up your reading speed (words per minute). Enter your reading speed on the graph on page 102.

Reading Time: Lesson 8

_____ : _____

Minutes　　　　*Seconds*

A Finding the Main Idea

One statement below expresses the main idea of the article. One statement is too general, or too broad. The other statement explains only part of the article; it is too narrow. Label the statements using the following key:

M—Main Idea   **B—Too Broad**   **N—Too Narrow**

_____ 1. A successful bull rider must stay seated on an agitated bull's back for at least eight seconds.

_____ 2. Old sports, such as bull riding, are still extremely popular.

_____ 3. Although bull riding is dangerous to riders and painful to bulls, it remains popular.

_____ Score 15 points for a correct M answer.

_____ Score 5 points for each correct B or N answer.

_____ **Total Score:** Finding the Main Idea

B Recalling Facts

How well do you remember the facts in the article? Put an X in the box next to the answer that correctly completes each statement about the article.

1. Every year, the deaths caused by bull riding average
   - ☐ a. one or two.
   - ☐ b. three or four.
   - ☐ c. at least five.

2. Bull rider Joshua "Cody" Brunner died when
   - ☐ a. the bull speared him with its horn.
   - ☐ b. his head violently struck against the bull's head.
   - ☐ c. a bull stepped on him after he dismounted.

3. A flank rope is tied tightly around the bull's
   - ☐ a. neck area.
   - ☐ b. belly at its hips.
   - ☐ c. upper chest.

4. Before the ride begins, bulls are sometimes
   - ☐ a. frightened by flashes of bright light.
   - ☐ b. hit with barbed-wire sticks.
   - ☐ c. prodded with an electric jolt.

5. Unlike male riders, female bull riders are allowed to
   - ☐ a. hold the rope with two hands, not one.
   - ☐ b. dismount after only six seconds.
   - ☐ c. wear a helmet.

Score 5 points for each correct answer.

_____ **Total Score:** Recalling Facts

C Making Inferences

When you combine your own experiences and information from a text to draw a conclusion that is not directly stated in that text, you are making an inference. Below are five statements that may or may not be inferences based on information in the article. Label the statements using the following key:

C—Correct Inference   **F—Faulty Inference**

_____ 1. If riders and fans knew that the bulls were in pain, they would no longer buy tickets to see bull riding.

_____ 2. Bull riding was started at a time when people did not think much about the comfort of the animal.

_____ 3. Most women who ride are glad that that the rules allow them to use two hands on the rope.

_____ 4. Medical teams are probably available at bull riding championships.

_____ 5. PETA and other animal rights groups are against harming animals for any professional sport or entertainment.

Score 5 points for each correct answer.

_____ **Total Score**: Making Inferences

D Using Words Precisely

Each numbered sentence below contains an underlined word or phrase from the article. Following the sentence are three definitions. One definition is closest to the meaning of the underlined word. One definition is opposite or nearly opposite. Label those two definitions using the following key. Do not label the remaining definition.

C—Closest   **O—Opposite or Nearly Opposite**

1. In the abstract, it sounds easy enough to do.

_____ a. in theory

_____ b. in the end

_____ c. in reality

2. Lee took his seat atop a bull named Chili in a claustrophobic gated steel chute barely big enough to hold bull and rider.

_____ a. likely to be remembered for a long time

_____ b. likely to cause comfort by creating a feeling of openness and freedom

_____ c. likely to cause fear by being small and closed in

3. It took Lee four months to recuperate sufficiently from brain surgery to ride again.

_____ a. calm down

_____ b. worsen

_____ c. recover

4. No one in the industry seems to question the sanity of riding on the back of an agitated bull.

_____ a. peaceful

_____ b. deeply distressed

_____ c. enormous

5. In many ways, bull riding is caught between two <u>contradictory</u> worlds.

_____ a. like-minded

_____ b. popular

_____ c. opposing

_____ Score 3 points for each correct C answer.

_____ Score 2 points for each correct O answer.

_____ **Total Score**: Using Words Precisely

Enter the four total scores in the spaces below, and add them together to find your Reading Comprehension Score. Then record your score on the graph on page 103.

Score	Question Type	Lesson 8
_____	Finding the Main Idea	
_____	Recalling Facts	
_____	Making Inferences	
_____	Using Words Precisely	
_____	**Reading Comprehension Score**	

Author's Approach

Put an X in the box next to the correct answer.

1. The main purpose of the first paragraph is to
   ☐ a. explain why bull riding is cruel to the bull.
   ☐ b. persuade the reader to try bull riding as a sport.
   ☐ c. describe the difficulty and dangers of bull riding.

2. From the statements below, choose the one that you believe the author would agree with.
   ☐ a. Bull riders are smarter, braver, and tougher than any other athletes.
   ☐ b. Bull riding should be against the law.
   ☐ c. The dangers that are part of bull riding are what make the sport attractive to many people.

3. Choose the statement below that is the weakest argument for bull riding.
   ☐ a. Riding the bull is over in just a few seconds.
   ☐ b. A few bull riders are killed every year.
   ☐ c. Bull riding is exciting and fun for fans.

4. Judging by statements from the article "Bull Riding: Ride or Run!," you can conclude that the author wants the reader to think that
   ☐ a. bull riding is not a dangerous sport after all.
   ☐ b. riders should not be surprised when they are injured.
   ☐ c. people ride bulls only because the sport pays well.

_____ Number of correct answers

Record your personal assessment of your work on the Critical Thinking Chart on page 104.

Summarizing and Paraphrasing

Put an X in the box next to the correct answer.

1. Choose the best one-sentence paraphrase for the following sentence from the article: "In addition to the extreme discomfort the strap causes, the bull's enraged bucking sometimes causes unintentional but severe injury to the animal."

☐ a. The strap is painful to the bull, and the bucking it causes sometimes injures the bull badly.

☐ b. Even though the strap hurts the bull, the sport would not be exciting without it.

☐ c. In addition to causing the bull pain, the strap may also cause the rider to be severely injured.

2. Below are summaries of the article. Choose the summary that says all the most important things about the article but in the fewest words.

☐ a. Although many people have been injured or killed while taking part in bull riding, most bull riders insist that those injuries are only freak accidents.

☐ b. When bull riders climb onto agitated bulls, they know that there is a chance for injury. Even so, riders enjoy the challenge, and fans reward them for their courage.

☐ c. Bull riding has been criticized for cruelty to bulls. The flank strap hurts the bulls and may lead to lasting injury.

_____ Number of correct answers

Record your personal assessment of your work on the Critical Thinking Chart on page 104.

Critical Thinking

Follow the directions provided for questions 1 and 3. Put an X next to the correct answer for the other questions.

1. For each statement below, write O if it expresses an opinion or write F if it expresses a fact.

_____ a. Animal rights groups should leave bull riders alone.

_____ b. Greyhound racing has been banned in all but a few states.

_____ c. Children as young as 12 years old enjoy riding bulls.

2. From the article, you can predict that

☐ a. bull riding will soon lose its popularity.

☐ b. within a few years, no one from animal rights groups will object to bull riding.

☐ c. Tammy Kelly will probably continue to ride bulls, even if she is injured by a bull.

3. Choose from the letters below to correctly complete the following statement. Write the letters on the lines.

On the positive side, _____, but on the negative side _____.

a. bull riders risk injury every time they climb onto a bull

b. bull riders can make a lot of money

c. women bull riders usually hold onto the rope with one hand, just like the men do

4. What was the cause of the death of rider Daniel Dopps?

☐ a. The weight of the bull crushed him.

☐ b. The bull he was riding tripped.

☐ c. He could not stay on the bull for eight seconds.

5. How is bull riding an example of the theme of this book?

☐ a. Bull riding is a sport that has been popular at rodeos for many years and is still popular today.

☐ b. Bull riding is a dangerous job that only a few daring people are willing to do.

☐ c. While some people like bull riding, others object to it.

_____ Number of correct answers

Record your personal assessment of your work on the Critical Thinking Chart on page 104.

Personal Response

What new question do you have about this topic?

_____

_____

_____

_____

Self-Assessment

From reading this article, I have learned

_____

_____

_____

_____

_____

_____

_____

_____

Astronaut Mechanics

Hanging in Space

Astronaut David A. Wolf installs a camera outside of the International Space Station. Wolf's space walk lasted six hours and four minutes.

What do you do with a bolt that won't loosen? For most people, whose feet are planted firmly on the ground, this is not a difficult problem. With enough lubricating oil and a little extra muscle, the bolt will eventually yield. But imagine trying to loosen a stubborn bolt while floating in space. Also keep in mind that if you can't loosen that bolt, the people you work for will lose $132 million. That was the situation facing astronaut mechanics John Grunsfeld and Andrew Feustel on May 15, 2009. The two men had left the space shuttle *Atlantis* and spacewalked to the Hubble Space Telescope, where they were trying to loosen a critical but reluctant bolt in order to take off an old camera and attach a new one. The new camera would allow the telescope to see even deeper into space. But this new camera, which cost $132 million to build, was worthless unless it could be installed.

2   Every astronaut faces hazards, of course, and they know there is no guarantee of a safe return to Earth. One example is the tragic explosion of the shuttle *Challenger* in 1986, which killed all seven people on board. Astronaut mechanics, however, face additional risks. To carry out repairs, they must spacewalk, which means leaving the relative safety of their spaceship and venturing weightless into silent, open space. Although they carry their own oxygen supply with them and are protected by high-pressure suits, many things can go wrong. In 2004 astronaut

mechanic Mike Fincke was just 14 minutes into a spacewalk mission to repair the International Space Station when oxygen suddenly began leaking out of his tank. A switch on his spacesuit had not been locked into its proper position. Fortunately, Fincke was close enough to the shuttle to get back inside safely, but it was a sobering reminder of the dangers of his job.

3   Another danger that these mechanics encounter comes from the extreme temperatures of space. Touching something that has been directly exposed to the sun's rays for a substantial period of time could burn an astronaut badly, even when he or she is wearing highly protective gloves. Conversely, working where the sun has not shone for a long time could result in frostbite. There also is the possibility of damage to the spacesuit that could happen if an astronaut mechanic brushes against a sharp edge of the spacecraft or space shuttle. Damage to the spacesuit could also occur if he or she is hit by floating debris. Outer space is littered with "micrometeoroids" — bits of rock and metal from asteroid collisions in the solar system. If any little thing were to puncture a spacesuit, the astronaut's entire oxygen

supply would be at risk. Depending on how many layers of the suit were torn and the size of the tear, the oxygen could either leak slowly or escape too rapidly for the astronaut to return to safety. This possibility was a special concern for John Grunsfeld and Andrew Feustel, since the Hubble Space Telescope was in a 350-mile high orbit around Earth. This orbit zone is loaded not only with micrometeoroids but with other debris from early satellites and discarded rocket launchers.

An astronaut mechanic makes repairs 350 miles above Earth while traveling at 18,000 miles per hour.

4 Grunsfeld and Feustel didn't spend much time reflecting on such risks, however. They focused on installing that new camera. They could do it only if they could get the bolt loose. Feustel tried a socket wrench, but it did nothing to budge the bolt. Grunsfeld went back to the shuttle and got a different tool, but that one didn't work, either. At that point, the two men had only one high-risk choice left. They would have to adjust the wrench to apply maximum pressure on the bolt. They had been warned against this move, since it could cause the bolt to snap off, making it impossible to remove the old camera.

5 "What are the implications if I over-torque and break the bolt?" Feustel asked himself as he began to twist with all his might.

6 Grunsfeld had just reminded him of the possible result when Feustel spoke again. "It turned," Feustel exclaimed. "It definitely turned." The crew back in the *Atlantis* and the people on Earth at Mission Control all let out a loud cheer as Feustel and Grunsfeld went about the job of replacing the camera.

7 In 2007 astronaut mechanic Scott Parazynski faced an even more dangerous situation. His job was to repair a ripped solar energy panel on the International Space Station. To fix it, Parazynski had to climb out on a 90-foot robotic arm. At this distance, he was more than 30 minutes from the space station's pressurized compartments. If something had gone wrong with Parazynski's air supply, he would have been too far away to make it back safely. Beyond that, the solar panel he had to fix was alive with more than 100 volts of electricity, so there was also the danger of electrocution if he touched the wrong part. As if that were not enough, the panel was bristly with sharp edges that easily could have punctured his space suit. Parazynski worked carefully and methodically for seven hours and 19 minutes to complete the necessary repairs.

8 Seemingly small mishaps and slip-ups can turn into major problems in space. In 2008 astronaut mechanic Heidemarie Stefanyshyn-Piper's tool bag slipped out of her hands during a spacewalk. She tried to grab it, but it floated away too quickly. The bag held $100,000 worth of equipment. "It was hardest coming back in and having to face everyone else," she said. In 2004 Russia's Alexander Kaleri was repairing the exterior of the International Space Station when moisture built up inside his helmet. He reported "full condensation," saying, "It's amazing. I have rain inside the helmet." In 2010, Douglas Wheelock and Tracy Caldwell Dyson spent more than eight hours outside of the space station trying to fix a hose that was leaking ammonia. After it was fixed, there was concern that their suits and equipment contained ammonia crystals. So before they could rest, they both had to go through a long drawn-out decontamination process.

9 Beyond all of these potential problems, astronaut mechanics may face at least one additional hazard that earthbound mechanics do not face. It may sound like science fiction, but some scientists worry that cosmic rays cause astronaut mechanics to grow old faster. There is some evidence suggesting that direct exposure to cosmic rays speeds up the aging process. Scientists think the spacecrafts protect astronauts from most cosmic rays, but that protection is missing during spacewalks. While scientists study the issue, most astronaut mechanics are thinking of more immediate problems. After all, they have enough real-time worries in their high-risk occupation as it is. ✴

If you have been timed while reading this article, enter your reading time below. Then turn to the Words-per-Minute Table on page 101 and look up your reading speed (words per minute). Enter your reading speed on the graph on page 102.

Reading Time: Lesson 9

_____ : _____

Minutes   *Seconds*

A Finding the Main Idea

One statement below expresses the main idea of the article. One statement is too general, or too broad. The other statement explains only part of the article; it is too narrow. Label the statements using the following key:

M—Main Idea   **B—Too Broad**   **N—Too Narrow**

_____ 1. Astronaut mechanics faced difficult problems replacing a camera on the Hubble Space Telescope.

_____ 2. Astronaut mechanics, who repair objects orbiting Earth, have a dangerous job.

_____ 3. Astronaut mechanics face many risks while making repairs outside the relative safety of their spaceships.

_____ Score 15 points for a correct M answer.

_____ Score 5 points for each correct B or N answer.

_____ **Total Score**: Finding the Main Idea

B Recalling Facts

How well do you remember the facts in the article? Put an X in the box next to the answer that correctly completes each statement about the article.

1. The name of the space shuttle that exploded in 1986 was
☐ a. _Atlantis._
☐ b. _Challenger._
☐ c. _Columbia._

2. Grunsfeld's and Feustel's last chance to repair the Hubble Space Telescope was to
☐ a. get a larger, heavier tool.
☐ b. apply maximum pressure to the bolt.
☐ c. use lubricating oil to loosen it.

3. Astronaut Scott Parazynski's mission in space was to
☐ a. remove an old camera and attach a new one.
☐ b. fix a 90-foot robotic arm.
☐ c. repair a ripped solar energy panel.

4. Astronaut Alexander Kaleri faced the problem of
☐ a. a leaking oxygen tank.
☐ b. moisture building up inside his helmet.
☐ c. possible contamination of his suit with ammonia crystals.

5. The tool bag that slipped out of astronaut Heidemarie Stefanyshyn-Piper's hands held equipment worth
☐ a. $90,000.
☐ b. $132 million.
☐ c. $100,000.

Score 5 points for each correct answer.

_____ **Total Score**: Recalling Facts

C Making Inferences

When you combine your own experiences and information from a text to draw a conclusion that is not directly stated in that text, you are making an inference. Below are five statements that may or may not be inferences based on information in the article. Label the statements using the following key:

C—Correct Inference   **F—Faulty Inference**

_____ 1. The space program costs many hundreds of millions of dollars.

_____ 2. A lot of work and care goes into the design of space suits.

_____ 3. Tools that astronaut mechanics use for repairs in space are exactly the same as tools used by mechanics on Earth.

_____ 4. Astronaut mechanics receive intensive training before going into space.

_____ 5. All of space is littered with floating debris.

Score 5 points for each correct answer.

_____ **Total Score**: Making Inferences

D Using Words Precisely

Each numbered sentence below contains an underlined word or phrase from the article. Following the sentence are three definitions. One definition is closest to the meaning of the underlined word. One definition is opposite or nearly opposite. Label those two definitions using the following key. Do not label the remaining definition.

C—Closest   **O—Opposite or Nearly Opposite**

1. With enough <u>lubricating</u> oil and a little extra muscle, the bolt will eventually yield.

_____ a. making slippery

_____ b. drying out

_____ c. not made from natural materials

2. The astronauts were trying to loosen a critical but <u>reluctant</u> bolt.

_____ a. eager

_____ b. unwilling

_____ c. broken

3. Mike Fincke received a <u>sobering</u> reminder of the dangers that astronaut mechanics face.

_____ a. unimportant

_____ b. cautious

_____ c. serious

4. Astronauts don't spend much time <u>reflecting</u> on the risks of their job.

_____ a. ignoring

_____ b. thinking about

_____ c. complaining about

5. The astronaut worked carefully and <u>methodically</u> to complete the necessary repairs.

_____ a. nervously

_____ b. inaccurately

_____ c. precisely

_____ Score 3 points for each correct C answer.

_____ Score 2 points for each correct O answer.

_____ **Total Score**: Using Words Precisely

Enter the four total scores in the spaces below, and add them together to find your Reading Comprehension Score. Then record your score on the graph on page 103.

Score	Question Type	Lesson 9
_____	Finding the Main Idea	
_____	Recalling Facts	
_____	Making Inferences	
_____	Using Words Precisely	
_____	**Reading Comprehension Score**	

Author's Approach

Put an X in the box next to the correct answer.

1. The author probably wrote this article to

☐ a. provide details of the mistakes made by the space program.

☐ b. discourage the reader from becoming an astronaut mechanic by describing the risks of the job.

☐ c. make the reader aware of the skill and courage of astronaut mechanics.

2. The article states, "If something had gone wrong with Parazynski's air supply, he would have been too far away to make it back safely." You can conclude from this statement that the author wants the reader to think that

☐ a. Parazynski was being irresponsible to go so far into space.

☐ b. Parazynski was exceptionally brave to go out so far into space.

☐ c. Parazynski had made a mistake and gone out too far into space.

3. In this article, "Seemingly small mishaps and slip-ups can turn into major problems in space" means

☐ a. astronauts are constantly making mistakes in space that range from little errors to huge miscalculations.

☐ b. there are no small problems in space, only major ones.

☐ c. problems that could be easily handled on Earth can become much harder to solve in space.

_____ Number of correct answers

Record your personal assessment of your work on the Critical Thinking Chart on page 104.

CRITICAL THINKING

Summarizing and Paraphrasing

Put an X in the box next to the correct answer for questions 1 and 2. Follow the directions provided for question 3.

1. Choose the best one-sentence paraphrase for the following sentence from the article: "There is some evidence suggesting that direct exposure to cosmic rays speeds up the aging process."

   ☐ a. There is proof that cosmic rays make some people age faster.

   ☐ b. There are some signs that indicate that cosmic rays might make people age faster.

   ☐ c. We know for a fact that cosmic rays speed up the rate at which people age.

2. Read the statement about the article below. Then read the paraphrase of that statement. Choose the reason that best tells why the paraphrase does not say the same thing as the statement.

   Statement: To fix it, Parazynski had to climb out on a 90-foot robotic arm.

   Paraphrase: Parazynski, who is 6 feet 2 inches tall, worked to repair a ripped solar energy panel at the end of a 90-foot robotic arm.

   ☐ a. Paraphrase says too much.

   ☐ b. Paraphrase doesn't say enough.

   ☐ c. Paraphrase doesn't agree with the statement.

3. Look for the important ideas and events in the first two paragraphs. Summarize those paragraphs in one or two sentences.

   _____

   _____

   _____

   _____

   _____ Number of correct answers

   Record your personal assessment of your work on the Critical Thinking Chart on page 104.

Critical Thinking

Follow the directions provided for questions 1, 2, and 5. Put an X in the box next to the correct answer for the other questions.

1. For each statement below, write O if it expresses an opinion or write F if it expresses a fact.

   _____ a. Being exposed to cosmic rays is the biggest hazard facing astronaut mechanics.

   _____ b. Micrometeoroids are bits of rock and metal from asteroid collisions in the solar system.

   _____ c. Astronaut mechanics carry their own oxygen supply on spacewalks.

2. Choose from the letters below to correctly complete the following statement. Write the letters on the lines.

   In the article, _____ and _____ are alike because they are hazards that astronaut mechanics must face.

   a. 90-foot robotic arms

   b. space debris

   c. extreme temperatures

CRITICAL THINKING

3. What caused Mike Fincke's oxygen tank to leak oxygen?

☐ a. a puncture

☐ b. a collision with floating debris

☐ c. an improperly locked switch

4. From the information in paragraph 6, you can conclude that the people at Mission Control

☐ a. had been keeping close track of the progress of Grunsfeld's and Feustel's mission.

☐ b. were shocked that Grunsfeld and Feustel were successful in their mission.

☐ c. had not been paying much attention to Grunsfeld's and Feustel's mission until there was a problem.

5. In which paragraph did you find your information or details to answer question 3?

_____

_____ Number of correct answers

Record your personal assessment of your work on the Critical Thinking Chart on page 104.

Personal Response

How do you think Heidemarie Stefanyshyn-Piper felt when her tool bag floated away?

_____

_____

_____

_____

Self-Assessment

I'm proud of how I answered question _____ in the _____ section because

_____

_____

_____

_____

_____

_____

_____

_____

MMA Fighters
Martial Arts Mash-Up

In the world of sports, there's tough, there's really tough, and then there's MMA-tough. For those who aren't familiar with MMA, it stands for "Mixed Martial Arts"—an outrageous blend of skill, ferocity, and violence. Developed in the 1990s, MMA features elements of judo, wrestling, boxing, and all-out street fighting. Name any kind of martial art, and you will see parts of it incorporated into MMA, from the Muay Thai fighting of Thailand to the Jiu Jitsu of Brazil. MMA goes by many names—ultimate fighting, extreme fighting, no-holds-barred fighting—but whatever it is called, the goal is to mimic real-life unarmed combat situations.

2 In an MMA fight, opponents meet in a ring or cage and try to beat each other into submission. The rules vary from league to league, but most fighters follow guidelines set down by the Ultimate Fighting Championship (UFC), the sport's dominant organization. UFC fighters are allowed to punch, kick, and put strangleholds on their opponents. They can stomp on each other's feet and throw elbows to the face and neck. They can jam a knee into an opponent's stomach, kick him in the liver, and hold him down while they pummel him in the face. In fact, the list of what UFC fighters can do

Thales Leites, right, from Brazil, and Anderson Silva, also from Brazil, battle during the Mixed Martial Arts middle-weight fight of the Ultimate Fighting Championship.

is so long that it is easier just to list what they *cannot* do. Head butting is not allowed. Neither is hair pulling nor punches to the back of the head. A fighter can't kick another fighter in the groin, gouge his eyes, or choke him in a way that cuts off his air supply. There are a few other rules as well, but you get the idea: ultimate fighting lets each fighter use his body in almost any way possible to defeat his opponent. This makes sense, since the concept of Mixed Martial Arts grew out of speculation about which kind of martial arts fighter would prevail on the street. If you make too many rules, you take the "street" out of the fight.

3   Most MMA fights consist of three five-minute rounds, with a one-minute rest period between each round. In any MMA fight, there are four routes to victory. One is to knock the opponent unconscious. A second is for a referee to declare a technical knockout (TKO). This occurs when, in the judgment of the referee, one fighter is unable to continue defending himself. A third way is for one fighter to concede, usually by tapping or verbally signaling defeat. This typically happens when a fighter is locked into a position from which he can't escape and he realizes that if he continues struggling he is likely to sustain serious injury. The final way, used if both fighters have completed all rounds, is for a panel of judges to declare a victor.

4   Because MMA can look a lot like a barroom brawl, you might think the sport takes nothing more than brute strength and an aggressive attitude. Those who have

risen to the top, however, maintain that nothing could be further from the truth. UFC heavyweight champ Fedor Emelianenko says, "My training is not simple. I believe I train harder than anyone else in the world." Famed MMA fighter and trainer Renzo Gracie acknowledges that at first glance, MMA fighters are simply trying to knock each other senseless. But, he insists their efforts go far beyond that. There's so much technique involved, Gracie says, that a good fight is more graceful than ballet. After studying the physics of the fighters'

movements, California State University professor Nancy Cheever agrees. Says Cheever, "It's very technical. It takes years and years of discipline to become an MMA fighter." Coach Pat Miletich describes the difference between boxing and MMA as the difference between checkers and chess. Because MMA combines so many moves from so many different traditions, he says it is like a tree with hundreds of branches. According to Miletich, "If I do one submission hold on you, you have three different ways to escape. That's three . . .

Mixed Martial Arts rules allow both grappling and striking techniques.

branches. And I have three moves off of each one of those branches. And then it just keeps going from there. It's very complex." Perhaps this complexity helps explain why so many athletes from other sports have been attracted to MMA. Mixed Martial Arts has among its ranks 14 former Olympians, 17 former NCAA wrestling champions, and dozens of former college or professional football players.

5   Although acting tough may not be the only thing you need to be a good MMA fighter, it is one of the prerequisites. After all, there is a reason why MMA fighters boast such nicknames as Rampage, the Monster, and the Axe Murderer. Even female fighters—yes, women can also be Mixed Martial Arts fighters—have ominous nicknames. How would you like to climb into the ring with Whiplash, Steel, or Cyborg? But, as Renzo Gracie puts it, "You cannot hide who you are once you step on the ring." A nasty attitude and a slick nickname provide some cover, but if a fighter is afraid, it shows. You have to back up what you set up.

6   Not everyone is a fan of MMA. Critics decry it as cruel, like "human cockfighting,"

pointing out that it has been linked to brain damage and premature death. One study has shown that 40 percent of all MMA fights end with at least one injured fighter. These injuries may range from facial cuts to severe concussions or worse. Dr. Vivienne Nathanson, head of ethics and science at the British Medical Association, is adamant that MMA fighting "can cause traumatic brain injury, joint injuries, and fractures." Declares Nathanson, "This kind of competition hardly constitutes a sport—the days of gladiator fights are over, and we should not be looking to resurrect them."

7   Many detractors point to Sam Vasquez, who collapsed during an MMA fight in Houston in 2007. Vasquez was rushed to the hospital, where doctors found he was bleeding in his brain. He underwent two surgeries but suffered a massive stroke and died without ever making it home to his wife and seven-year-old son.

8   Despite the risks and the criticism, Mixed Martial Arts is growing in popularity. In 2007 the average UFC bout brought in ticket sales of $2.8 million. That same year, the sport generated $200 million in pay-per-view revenues.

Predicts Nancy Cheever, "It's eventually going to become an Olympic sport." Depending on your point of view, MMA can be considered a fun, full-contact competition, challenging hand-to-hand combat, or a barbaric blood bath. In any case, for better or for worse, it is probably the only sport where avoiding contact actually is grounds for a foul. ✳

If you have been timed while reading this article, enter your reading time below. Then turn to the Words-per-Minute Table on page 101 and look up your reading speed (words per minute). Enter your reading speed on the graph on page 102.

Reading Time: Lesson 10

_____ : _____

Minutes   Seconds

A Finding the Main Idea

One statement below expresses the main idea of the article. One statement is too general, or too broad. The other statement explains only part of the article; it is too narrow. Label the statements using the following key:

M—Main Idea   **B—Too Broad**   **N—Too Narrow**

_____ 1. Mixed Martial Arts is a very violent style of fighting.

_____ 2. Mixed Martial Arts fighters train hard but are often hurt in their short action-packed fights.

_____ 3. Mixed Martial Arts is a popular, violent style of unarmed fighting that allows almost any kind of fighting move.

_____ Score 15 points for a correct M answer.

_____ Score 5 points for each correct B or N answer.

_____ **Total Score**: Finding the Main Idea

B Recalling Facts

How well do you remember the facts in the article? Put an X in the box next to the answer that correctly completes each statement about the article.

1. According to the article, most MMA fighters follow guidelines set down by the
   - ☐ a. Ultimate Fighting Championship.
   - ☐ b. Universal Fighting Arts Organization.
   - ☐ c. World Martial Arts Organization.

2. One of the few moves that is not allowed in MMA fighting is
   - ☐ a. jamming a knee into an opponent's stomach.
   - ☐ b. pulling hair.
   - ☐ c. stomping on each other's feet.

3. Most MMA fights consist of
   - ☐ a. three five-minute rounds.
   - ☐ b. five three-minute rounds.
   - ☐ c. five five-minute rounds.

4. One study has shown that 40 percent of all MMA fights
   - ☐ a. give a fighter a concussion.
   - ☐ b. give a fighter joint injuries and fractures.
   - ☐ c. cause at least one fighter to be injured.

5. In 2007 the ticket sales for the average UFC fight were
   - ☐ a. $200 million.
   - ☐ b. more than $2 million.
   - ☐ c. about $8 million.

Score 5 points for each correct answer.

_____ **Total Score**: Recalling Facts

C Making Inferences

When you combine your own experiences and information from a text to draw a conclusion that is not directly stated in that text, you are making an inference. Below are five statements that may or may not be inferences based on information in the article. Label the statements using the following key:

C—Correct Inference   **F—Faulty Inference**

_____ 1. Most fans do not realize how violent MMA fighting is.

_____ 2. If MMA fighters had better training, no fighters would get hurt.

_____ 3. The panels of fight judges watch the fights intently.

_____ 4. Although there are women who are MMA fighters, most of the fighters are men.

_____ 5. All MMA fighters have nicknames.

Score 5 points for each correct answer.

_____ **Total Score**: Making Inferences

D Using Words Precisely

Each numbered sentence below contains an underlined word or phrase from the article. Following the sentence are three definitions. One definition is closest to the meaning of the underlined word. One definition is opposite or nearly opposite. Label those two definitions using the following key. Do not label the remaining definition.

C—Closest   **O—Opposite or Nearly Opposite**

1. Name any kind of martial art, and you will see parts of it incorporated into MMA.

   _____ a. excluded from

   _____ b. blended into

   _____ c. similar to

2. MMA grew out of speculation about which kind of martial arts fighter would prevail on the street.

   _____ a. disappoint

   _____ b. lose out

   _____ c. prove superior

3. Although acting tough may not be the only thing you need to be a good fighter, it is one of the prerequisites.

   _____ a. requirements

   _____ b. characteristics

   _____ c. options

4. Even female fighters have ominous nicknames.

   _____ a. happy

   _____ b. menacing

   _____ c. bizarre

5. Critics <u>decry</u> MMA fights as cruel, like "human cockfighting."

_____ a. condemn

_____ b. describe

_____ c. praise

_____ Score 3 points for each correct C answer.

_____ Score 2 points for each correct O answer.

_____ **Total Score**: Using Words Precisely

Enter the four total scores in the spaces below, and add them together to find your Reading Comprehension Score. Then record your score on the graph on page 103.

Score	Question Type	Lesson 10
_____	Finding the Main Idea	
_____	Recalling Facts	
_____	Making Inferences	
_____	Using Words Precisely	
_____	**Reading Comprehension Score**	

Author's Approach

Put an X in the box next to the correct answer.

1. The author uses the first sentence of the article to

☐ a. inform the reader about the aims of MMA.

☐ b. describe the qualities of MMA fighters.

☐ c. compare MMA and other sports.

2. Choose the statement below that best explains how the author addresses the article's opposing points of view.

☐ a. A good fight is more graceful than ballet.

☐ b. MMA takes more than brute strength and an aggressive attitude.

☐ c. MMA can be considered a fun, full-contact competition, challenging hand-to-hand combat, or a barbaric blood bath.

3. The author probably wrote this article to

☐ a. offer a balanced view of MMA fighting.

☐ b. encourage readers to attend an MMA fight.

☐ c. persuade readers that MMA is brutal and dangerous.

4. The sentence "Coach Pat Miletich describes the difference between boxing and MMA as the difference between checkers and chess," means the coach thinks

☐ a. boxing is simple compared to MMA, just as checkers is a simple game compared to chess.

☐ b. boxing and MMA are very similar sports, just as checkers and chess are similar games.

☐ c. both boxing and checkers are boring, while MMA and chess are exciting.

_____ Number of correct answers

Record your personal assessment of your work on the Critical Thinking Chart on page 104.

CRITICAL THINKING

Summarizing and Paraphrasing

Put an X in the box next to the correct answer.

1. Choose the best one-sentence paraphrase for the following sentence from the article: "If you make too many rules, you take the 'street' out of the fight."

☐ a.   Street fights do not have any rules.

☐ b.   A fight with many rules becomes unlike a real-life fight.

☐ c.   A fight without any rules is too dangerous.

2. Read the statement from the article below. Then read the paraphrase of that statement. Choose the reason that best tells why the paraphrase does not say the same thing as the statement.

Statement: It takes years and years of discipline to become an MMA fighter.

Paraphrase: Anyone who practices for years and years can become an MMA fighter.

☐ a.   Paraphrase says too much.

☐ b.   Paraphrase doesn't say enough.

☐ c.   Paraphrase doesn't agree with the statement.

3. Below are summaries of the article. Choose the summary that says all the most important things about the article but in the fewest words.

☐ a.   MMA is a violent, skillful style of unarmed fighting that has both critics and supporters.

☐ b.   Attracting athletes from various sports, MMA is a style of fighting with few rules.

☐ c.   MMA is a form of fighting that includes moves from other types of martial arts. It is very brutal but very popular.

_____ Number of correct answers

Record your personal assessment of your work on the Critical Thinking Chart on page 104.

Critical Thinking

Follow the directions provided for questions 1 and 3. Put an X next to the correct answer for the other questions.

1. For each statement below, write O if it expresses an opinion or write F if it expresses a fact.

_____ a.   Not everyone is a fan of MMA.

_____ b.   In an MMA fight, opponents meet in a ring and try to beat each other into submission.

_____ c.   This kind of competition hardly constitutes a sport.

2. From the article, you can predict that

☐ a.   more rules will be imposed on MMA fights.

☐ b.   people will continue to have opposing views of MMA.

☐ c.   because it is so violent, MMA fighting will be banned.

3. Choose from the letters below to correctly complete the following statement. Write the letters on the lines.

   In the article, _____ and _____ are alike because they are moves not allowed in MMA fights.

   a. head butting

   b. throwing punches to the back of the head

   c. putting strangleholds on opponents

4. Of the following theme categories, which would this story fit into?

   ☐ a. Customs and Traditions

   ☐ b. Women in Sports

   ☐ c. Extreme Sports

5. From the information in paragraph 4, you can conclude that

   ☐ a. MMA training takes time, effort, and dedication.

   ☐ b. the best MMA fighters are former Olympians.

   ☐ c. training for MMA fights is a recent development.

_____ Number of correct answers

Record your personal assessment of your work on the Critical Thinking Chart on page 104.

Personal Response

What was most surprising or interesting to you about this article?

_____

_____

_____

_____

Self-Assessment

When reading this article, I was having trouble with

_____

_____

_____

_____

_____

_____

_____

_____

_____

_____

CRITICAL THINKING

Compare and Contrast

Think about the articles you have read in Unit Two. Choose three subjects that you would like to learn more about. Write the titles of the articles in the first column of the chart below. Use information you learned from the articles to fill in the empty boxes in the chart.

Title	What facts or ideas had you known about the job before reading the article?	Which ideas from the article were new to you?	Which ideas made you curious to learn more?

The subject I'm most interested in learning more about is _____. The main thing I'd like to find out is

_____

_____.

Words-per-Minute Table

Unit Two

Directions If you were timed while reading an article, refer to the Reading Time you recorded in the box at the end of the article. Use this words-per-minute table to determine your reading speed for that article. Then plot your reading speed on the graph on page 102.

Lesson	6	7	8	9	10	
No. of Words	1133	1121	1051	1118	1106	Seconds
1:30	755	747	701	745	737	90
1:40	680	673	631	671	664	100
1:50	618	611	573	610	603	110
2:00	567	561	526	559	553	120
2:10	523	517	485	516	510	130
2:20	486	480	450	479	474	140
2:30	453	448	420	447	442	150
2:40	425	420	394	419	415	160
2:50	400	396	371	395	390	170
3:00	378	374	350	373	369	180
3:10	358	354	332	353	349	190
3:20	340	336	315	335	332	200
3:30	324	320	300	319	316	210
3:40	309	306	287	305	302	220
3:50	296	292	274	292	289	230
4:00	283	280	263	280	277	240
4:10	272	269	252	268	265	250
4:20	261	259	243	258	255	260
4:30	252	249	234	248	246	270
4:40	243	240	225	240	237	280
4:50	234	232	217	231	229	290
5:00	227	224	210	224	221	300
5:10	219	217	203	216	214	310
5:20	212	210	197	210	207	320
5:30	206	204	191	203	201	330
5:40	200	198	185	197	195	340
5:50	194	192	180	192	190	350
6:00	189	187	175	186	184	360
6:10	184	182	170	181	179	370
6:20	179	177	166	177	175	380
6:30	174	172	162	172	170	390
6:40	170	168	158	168	166	400
6:50	166	164	154	164	162	410
7:00	162	160	150	160	158	420
7:10	158	156	147	156	154	430
7:20	155	153	143	152	151	440
7:30	151	149	140	149	147	450
7:40	148	146	137	146	144	460
7:50	145	143	134	143	141	470
8:00	142	140	131	140	138	480

Minutes and Seconds

Plotting Your Progress: Reading Speed

Unit Two

Directions If you were timed while reading an article, write your words-per-minute rate for that article in the box under the number of the lesson. Then plot your reading speed on the graph by putting a small X on the line directly above the number of the lesson, across from the number of words per minute you read. As you mark your speed for each lesson, graph your progress by drawing a line to connect the Xs.

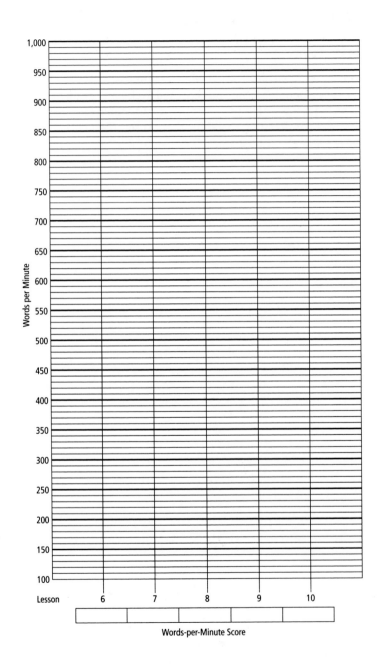

Words-per-Minute Score

Plotting Your Progress: Reading Comprehension

Unit Two

Directions Write your Reading Comprehension score for each lesson in the box under the number of the lesson. Then plot your score on the graph by putting a small X on the line directly above the number of the lesson and across from the score you earned. As you mark your score for each lesson, graph your progress by drawing a line to connect the Xs.

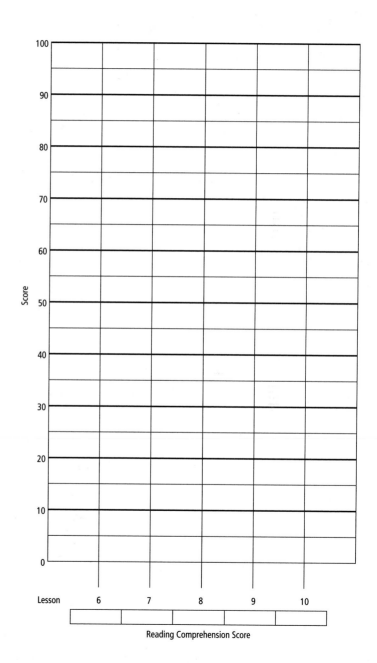

Reading Comprehension Score

Plotting Your Progress: Critical Thinking

Unit Two

Directions Work with your teacher to evaluate your responses to the Critical Thinking questions for each lesson. Then fill in the appropriate spaces in the chart below. For each lesson and each type of Critical Thinking question, do the following: Mark a minus sign (–) in the box to indicate areas in which you feel you could improve. Mark a plus sign (+) to indicate areas in which you feel you did well. Mark a minus-slash-plus sign (–/+) to indicate areas in which you had mixed success. Then write any comments you have about your performance, including ideas for improvement.

Lesson	Author's Approach	Summarizing and Paraphrasing	Critical Thinking
6			
7			
8			
9			
10			

Unit Three

Pirate Chasers

Crime Waves on the High Seas

Pirate gangs attack oil tankers and cargo ships from speedboats that are launched from a "mother ship."

Piracy has changed a lot since the days of Blackbeard and Captain Kidd. In those days, pirates roamed the seas in sailing ships that weighed hundreds of tons, with dozens of smoking cannons on deck. Pirates were famous for swashbuckling fights on blood-soaked decks, forcing victims to walk the plank, and making off with chests of jewels and gold coins. Today's pirates are a different breed altogether. They are more likely to attack in a small speedboat, armed with cell phones and machine guns, and they are more likely to announce their presence with a grenade launcher than with a skull-and-crossbones flag. Luckily, the defense against pirates has also changed a lot. So although the incidence of piracy has risen dramatically over the last 20 years, so has the sophistication and determination of pirate chasers.

2   Modern piracy is the result of many converging forces. For one thing, the opportunities for pirates are increasingly attractive. Thanks to increased technology, giant freighters can now operate with smaller and smaller crews. That means there are fewer people on hand to protect a ship and its cargo. Meanwhile, countries around the world have reduced their naval forces, so there are fewer ships policing the seas. Add to that the fact that pirates have the same access to high-tech weapons and tracking systems as anyone else. Factor in desperation and greed and you've got a pirate attack waiting to happen.

3   Today's pirates most often strike in the waters near Malaysia, Bangladesh, and Somalia, so that is where pirate chasers are typically stationed. These chasers are specialists who know how to work in small teams to carry out dangerous missions where there's no guarantee of success—or even survival. Sometimes they are part of government forces or multinational groups. They may be part of the Marines, the Navy, or a special military task force. In that case, their ships are usually decked out with everything from long-range acoustic devices to helicopter pads to surface-to-surface missiles. In other cases, pirate chasers are private security forces that can be called in at a moment's notice by a ship in trouble. These private forces may not be so heavily armed, but they are composed of individuals with backgrounds in military Special Forces. This means they have been trained in reconnaissance, surveillance, guerilla warfare, and counter-terrorism.

Many experts believe that poverty and a weak Somali government have created conditions that have resulted in piracy.

4   Such training is essential to success, according to John Dalby, founder of a private anti-piracy force headquartered in England. Many ship owners still believe that modern pirates are a bunch of fishermen with a loose plan and some AK-47 rifles. "This is serious stuff, now," says Dalby. "These guys are trained, and it's extremely well coordinated—and funded." John Burnett, author of the book *Dangerous Waters*, would agree, calling today's pirates "brutal, ruthless, and cold blooded." Examples of their brazen attacks include the 1999 hijacking of a cargo ship headed from Indonesia to Japan. As the ship cruised through the Malacca Strait, 15 men in high-speed boats suddenly appeared, surrounding the vessel. The unarmed crew of 17 had no way to fight back. The pirates boarded the ship, set the crew adrift in lifeboats, and took off with almost $15 million worth of aluminum in the ship's hold. By 2010, pirates off the coast of Somalia were making off with $100 million per year.

5   In the face of such rampant attacks, what do pirate chasers do? Not surprisingly, they want the details to remain secret so they can keep the pirates guessing. Still, some facts are clear. Pirate chasers do most of their riskiest work from 1 a.m. to 6 a.m. The darkness of those hours offers them cover so they can move toward a pirated ship unseen. In addition, that is when there is the greatest chance that at least some of the pirates are sleeping, with only a few keeping watch. Sometimes pirate chasers sneak up next to a hijacked ship, attach a satellite tracking device, and then disappear back into the night. They track the ship until it docks in some distant harbor, where ground forces can move in to recapture the cargo. In other cases, they mount a head-on attack while the hijacked ship is still at sea.

6   One such sea battle came on May 6, 2010, when a group of pirates carrying automatic weapons took command of a Russian oil tanker off the coast of Somalia. Russia asked its Marines to mount a counterattack in an effort to rescue the lives of the 23 crew members on board and the $50 million worth of oil. Late that night, a team of Russian Marines sprang into action. Some climbed aboard a helicopter so that they could come at the pirates from the air. Meanwhile, a second group of Marines set out in small boats, slipping through the water toward the sides of the tanker. If all went well, both groups would make it onto the ship simultaneously and overpower the pirates. But every pirate chaser who set out that night knew that things don't always unfold as planned. They all expected that the pirates, edgy and sleep-deprived, would be quick to shoot.

7   The drama unfolded over the course of three hours. In an impressive display of stealth and skill, both groups of Marines made it onto the tanker as planned. Some lowered themselves by rope from the helicopter onto the oil tanker's deck. The others scaled the sides of the ship from their small boats. Once on deck, they faced a 22-minute gunfight with the pirates. By the time it was over, one of the pirates was dead and the rest had been subdued. Amazingly, not a single Marine was killed and none of the crew members were injured. The president of Russia summed it up this way: "It was sharp, professional, and quick."

8   Stories like these confirm that pirates can be defeated. Not every mission ends so successfully, but the numbers indicate that the chasers are making progress. Ten years ago, one in three Somali pirate attacks was successful; today only one in ten succeeds. The war against piracy is far from over, so if a life of high adventure and high risks appeals to you, this is one career to consider. Just keep in mind this warning from John Dalby: "There's nothing pleasant about this business. You do run the risk of being killed." ✳

If you have been timed while reading this article, enter your reading time below. Then turn to the Words-per-Minute Table on page 147 and look up your reading speed (words per minute). Enter your reading speed on the graph on page 148.

Reading Time: Lesson 11

_____ : _____
Minutes   Seconds

A Finding the Main Idea

One statement below expresses the main idea of the article. One statement is too general, or too broad. The other statement explains only part of the article; it is too narrow. Label the statements using the following key:

M—Main Idea　　**B—Too Broad**　　**N—Too Narrow**

_____ 1. In May 2010, Russian Marines won a 22-minute gunfight with pirates who had seized a Russian oil tanker off the coast of Somalia.

_____ 2. It may be difficult to believe, but the modern world has recently seen an increase in both pirates and pirate chasers.

_____ 3. A combination of daring and military training is what's needed to chase down and defeat modern pirates who prey on defenseless cargo ships on the open sea.

_____ Score 15 points for a correct M answer.

_____ Score 5 points for each correct B or N answer.

_____ **Total Score:** Finding the Main Idea

B Recalling Facts

How well do you remember the facts in the article? Put an X in the box next to the answer that correctly completes each statement about the article.

1. Modern pirates are most likely to attack from
   ☐ a. small speedboats.
   ☐ b. large cruise ships.
   ☐ c. giant sailing ships.

2. Pirate chasers are most often stationed off the coasts of
   ☐ a. South Africa, Namibia, and Angola.
   ☐ b. England, Ireland, and Scotland.
   ☐ c. Bangladesh, Somalia, and Malaysia.

3. In 1999, pirates hijacked a cargo ship sailing from Indonesia to Japan and then
   ☐ a. sank the ship after stealing its cargo.
   ☐ b. set the crew adrift on the sea in small lifeboats.
   ☐ c. killed the entire crew.

4. Pirate chasers like to do much of their work between
   ☐ a. 10 p.m. and 3 a.m.
   ☐ b. 1 a.m. and 6 a.m.
   ☐ c. 9 a.m. and 5 p.m.

5. Somali pirates are now successful at the rate of about
   ☐ a. one out of every three attacks.
   ☐ b. one out of every eight attacks.
   ☐ c. one out of every ten attacks.

Score 5 points for each correct answer.

_____ **Total Score:** Recalling Facts

C | Making Inferences

When you combine your own experiences and information from a text to draw a conclusion that is not directly stated in that text, you are making an inference. Below are five statements that may or may not be inferences based on information in the article. Label the statements using the following key:

C—Correct Inference   **F—Faulty Inference**

_____ 1. The best pirate chaser would be someone who likes to work alone.

_____ 2. Around 30 years ago, cargo ships were attacked by pirates only rarely.

_____ 3. Even if most crews were armed, they probably could not win in a battle with pirates.

_____ 4. If you were set adrift in a lifeboat in the ocean, you could count on being rescued eventually.

_____ 5. Thanks to modern communications, today's pirates probably spend less time looking for a ship to attack than pirates of old spent.

Score 5 points for each correct answer.

_____ **Total Score**: Making Inferences

D | Using Words Precisely

Each numbered sentence below contains an underlined word or phrase from the article. Following the sentence are three definitions. One definition is closest to the meaning of the underlined word. One definition is opposite or nearly opposite. Label those two definitions using the following key. Do not label the remaining definition.

C—Closest   **O—Opposite or Nearly Opposite**

1. Modern piracy is the result of many <u>converging</u> forces.

    _____ a. complicated

    _____ b. coming together

    _____ c. drawing apart

2. <u>Factor in</u> desperation and greed, and you've got a pirate attack waiting to happen.

    _____ a. take into account

    _____ b. refuse to consider

    _____ c. attempt to accomplish

3. In the face of such <u>rampant</u> attacks, what do pirate chasers do?

    _____ a. limited or contained

    _____ b. cruel

    _____ c. out-of-control

4. If all went well, both groups would make it onto the ship <u>simultaneously</u> and overpower the pirates.

    _____ a. at the same time

    _____ b. on time

    _____ c. one at a time

5. By the time it was over, one of the pirates was dead and the rest had been <u>subdued</u>.

_____ a. arrested

_____ b. victorious

_____ c. conquered

_____ Score 3 points for each correct C answer.

_____ Score 2 points for each correct O answer.

_____ **Total Score:** Using Words Precisely

Enter the four total scores in the spaces below, and add them together to find your Reading Comprehension Score. Then record your score on the graph on page 149.

Score	Question Type	Lesson 11
_____	Finding the Main Idea	
_____	Recalling Facts	
_____	Making Inferences	
_____	Using Words Precisely	
_____	**Reading Comprehension Score**	

Author's Approach

Put an X in the box next to the correct answer.

1. The main purpose of the first paragraph is to

☐ a. explain why piracy is on the rise today.

☐ b. compare historical and modern pirates.

☐ c. make modern pirates sound like heroes.

2. What does the speaker imply with this statement: "Many ship owners still believe that modern pirates are a bunch of fishermen with a loose plan and some AK-47 rifles"?

☐ a. Ship owners think that modern pirates should go back to fishing for a living.

☐ b. Ship owners think that modern pirates are clever.

☐ c. Ship owners don't take the threat of pirates seriously enough.

3. Considering the statement from the article, "Just keep in mind this warning from John Dalby: 'There's nothing pleasant about this business. You do run the risk of being killed,'" you can conclude that the author wants the reader to think that pirate chasing

☐ a. would be a satisfying and enjoyable job.

☐ b. is not an easy or safe occupation.

☐ c. is a job that the author would secretly like to try.

4. Which of the following phrases from the article best describes the Russian Marines who defeated pirates in May 2010?

☐ a. sharp, professional, and quick

☐ b. brutal, ruthless, and cold blooded

☐ c. edgy and sleep-deprived

_____ Number of correct answers

Record your personal assessment of your work on the Critical Thinking Chart on page 150.

Summarizing and Paraphrasing

Follow the directions provided for question 1. Put an X in the box next to the correct answer for question 2.

1. Complete the following one-sentence summary of the article using the lettered phrases from the phrase bank below. Write the letters on the lines.

> **Phrase Bank:**
> a. an example of a successful operation by pirate chasers
> b. the skills and tactics of pirate chasers
> c. the reasons why piracy is on the rise today

The article "Pirate Chasers" begins with _____, goes on to describe _____, and ends with _____.

2. Read the statement from the article below. Then read the paraphrase of that statement. Choose the reason that best tells why the paraphrase does not say the same thing as the statement.

Statement: They [pirate chasers] track the ship until it docks in some distant harbor, where ground forces can move in to recapture the cargo.

Paraphrase: Using tracking devices, pirate chasers can follow a ship to a distant port and attack the pirates there.

☐ a. Paraphrase says too much.

☐ b. Paraphrase doesn't say enough.

☐ c. Paraphrase doesn't agree with the statement.

_____ Number of correct answers

Record your personal assessment of your work on the Critical Thinking Chart on page 150.

Critical Thinking

Follow the directions provided for question 2. Put an X next to the correct answer for the other questions.

1. Which of the following statements from the article is an opinion rather than a fact?

☐ a. The drama unfolded over the course of three hours.

☐ b. Once on deck, they faced a 22-minute gunfight with the pirates.

☐ c. "It was sharp, professional, and quick."

2. Using what you know about pirates of the past and what is told about today's pirates in the article, name three ways pirates of the past are similar to today's pirates and three ways they are different from today's pirates. Cite the paragraph number(s) where you found details in the article to support your conclusions.

Similarities

_____

_____

_____

Differences

_____

_____

_____

3. What is one effect of increased technology aboard freighters?

☐ a. Pirates have become more desperate and ruthless.

☐ b. Fewer crew members are available to protect the freighters.

☐ c. Crew members are more confident that they can defend their ships against pirates.

CRITICAL THINKING

4. How is "Pirate Chasers" related to the theme of *Mavericks*?

☐ a. Pirate chasing is both unusual and dangerous.

☐ b. Pirate chasers are usually either part of a government military task force or a private security force.

☐ c. Pirate chasers must be well-trained and coordinated.

5. What did you have to do to answer question 3?

☐ a. find a contrast (how things are different)

☐ b. find an effect (something that happened)

☐ c. find an opinion (what someone thinks about something)

_____ Number of correct answers

Record your personal assessment of your work on the Critical Thinking Chart on page 150.

Personal Response

How would you feel if you were a crew member on a cargo ship and saw a group of pirates speeding toward you?

_____

_____

_____

_____

Self-Assessment

Before reading this article, I already knew

_____

_____

_____

_____

_____

_____

_____

_____

Ranchers

At Home on the Range

Ranchers traditionally herd their horses and mules back and forth between winter feeding pastures in the lowlands and summer ranges in the highlands.

Who wouldn't want to be a rancher? As a rancher, you aren't corralled at a desk for eight or more hours a day. You don't have to drive through rush hour, ride a bus, or take a subway to work. At daybreak, you step out onto the porch and look across acres of landscape: birds are skimming the skies, bees are buzzing the flowers, and—what are those dark clouds over the ridge? Depending on what part of the country your ranch is in, that growing deep-gray mass above you could mean a thunderstorm, a snowstorm, or maybe even a hailstorm. Whatever it is, you'd better put down your coffee cup and get to work; you'll be busy now until nightfall. Have a nice day!

2   In some ways, cattle ranching in the United States has not changed a lot since the mid-1800s when settlers claimed thousands of acres of wide-open Western territory. Cowboys built fences, raised cattle, and brought their cattle to market. Ranchers then and now know that natural disasters such as drought, floods, hailstorms, and insect outbreaks literally come with the territory. Technological advances have made the day-to-day tasks of raising livestock easier, but there are still many possible problems that make ranching a difficult and often dangerous job. In fact, in some cases, it is the technology that causes the problems.

3   Everywhere a rancher looks, potential hazards loom because ranchers often work with very large and complex machinery.

When things go wrong, they often go spectacularly wrong. One rancher, for example, was killed when the attachment he was putting onto his tractor suddenly shifted, crushing him between it and the tractor. Another died after the bulldozer he was using to clear some land slid backward down a slope and rolled on top of him. Yet another died when a high-pressure irrigation line broke and water shot into his eye with such force that it burst an artery in his eye. Beyond the dangers posed by equipment, ranchers often must spray their fields with toxic pesticides, which can cause a wide variety of health risks for the animals and the humans.

4   The animals come with their own set of hazards. Ranchers are skilled at handling animals, of course, but at times, unpredictable animal behavior can create sudden chaos. North Dakota rancher Gary Skarda knew animals could be impulsive, but he didn't think he was buying trouble when, in April 2009, he purchased a six-year-old horse advertised as gentle and broken. Skarda uses horses on his ranch because they are better than all-terrain vehicles when working around livestock. "Horses are quieter around cattle," he said, adding, "and you don't want to work bulls with a four-wheeler." Skarda mounted his new horse a few times without any sign of

This farmer is feeding her cows on a free-range cattle ranch in Petaluma, California.

trouble, so one day he decided to use his new mount to check on his cattle. Skarda had been riding horses all his life and had even competed in rodeo events, so he knew how to handle all kinds of horses. This time, however, even his vast experience was not enough to keep him safe.

5   Skarda hadn't quite put his foot into the stirrups when the horse, for no apparent reason, suddenly reared up and began bucking. Skarda did his best to control the crazed horse, but it pulled the reins from his hands and threw him onto the ground. "The horse blew my foot out of the stirrup, so I couldn't lock my legs on the horse's side," Skarda later said. "I've never been thrown so hard in all my life." The fall broke his pelvis in two places and also his right hip and several ribs. He bled internally for 20 days and spent 22 days in the hospital before he was able to return home to begin his recovery.

6   Like horses, bulls can very quickly become dangerous, as Texas rancher and Grammy award-winning singer Lyle Lovett learned in 2002. Lovett was present when his uncle tried to control a bull that had broken loose. The bull flipped Lovett's uncle to the ground and then turned on Lovett, who was rushing to his uncle's aid. The animal stomped on Lovett's leg, breaking the bone into 20 pieces. Luckily, both Lovett and his uncle recovered, but it was a reminder of just how quickly violence can enter a rancher's life.

7   Besides the constant threat of stampedes, stompings, floods, and famine, ranchers also

live at the mercy of many unseen forces. For example, diseases can decimate herds in a very short time. A significant drop in market price can wipe out an entire year's profit in a single keystroke. Even less dire circumstances can take their toll; on any given day, a machine could break down or an animal could break a leg or have difficulty giving birth. All of this stress and uncertainty goes a long way toward explaining why, in one national survey of 130 occupations, ranchers ranked high in terms of stress-related illnesses such as heart disease, high blood pressure, and ulcers.

8   Given all of this, it is reasonable to ask why ranchers do it. The answer, for many of them, is that ranching is more than an occupation: it is a way of life. No matter how bad things get, these people wouldn't dream of doing anything else. Pat Litton is one such rancher. She operated a 23,000-acre ranch in Wyoming for more than 50 years. During that time, she lived through the death of her husband and her son in separate truck accidents. She also lived through the worst weather that nature could throw at her. Litton struggled to keep her ranch going through the droughts that parched her land and the floods that threatened to sweep everything away. In the winter of 1973, a fierce blizzard struck. It came at the worst possible time, because Litton's two thousand head of sheep, all freshly sheared, were out in the open, as were her two hundred cows. "After the blizzard I had about eight hundred head of sheep and maybe half of my cows left," she

said. The storm almost wiped her out financially, but she refused to give up, rebuilding her supply of livestock and carrying on as stoically as ever.

9   Did she ever think about packing it in and moving to the city? "It never occurred to me to quit," Litton said. "This ranch is my life. It's my dream. It's what keeps my heart pumping and my blood pumping. I'll stand on this land until the day I die." Young people are not exempt from having strong emotional ties to ranching. Jen Johnson and her brother Will left the family's ranch, but they returned a few years later with university degrees and new ideas about how to provide for it through land management and conservation. "I don't want to sound too boastful," Will said, "but I expect big things from us." Who wouldn't want to be a rancher? For many, there is no choice; it's just simply the way it is. ✷

If you have been timed while reading this article, enter your reading time below. Then turn to the Words-per-Minute Table on page 147 and look up your reading speed (words per minute). Enter your reading speed on the graph on page 148.

Reading Time: Lesson 12

_____ : _____

Minutes   *Seconds*

A | Finding the Main Idea

One statement below expresses the main idea of the article. One statement is too general, or too broad. The other statement explains only part of the article; it is too narrow. Label the statements using the following key:

M—Main Idea   **B—Too Broad**   **N—Too Narrow**

_____ 1. To some people, ranching may seem easy and safe, but in reality it is quite a dangerous occupation.

_____ 2. Although ranchers face danger from a variety of sources, including machinery, animals, and weather, many ranchers find it to be a satisfying occupation.

_____ 3. One danger of ranching can be seen in the case of a rancher who was killed when the attachment he was putting onto his tractor suddenly shifted and crushed him.

_____ Score 15 points for a correct M answer.

_____ Score 5 points for each correct B or N answer.

_____ **Total Score:** Finding the Main Idea

B | Recalling Facts

How well do you remember the facts in the article? Put an X in the box next to the answer that correctly completes each statement about the article.

1. In a terrible accident, a rancher's artery burst when
   ☐ a. a bulldozer rolled over him.
   ☐ b. an irrigation line broke and sprayed him.
   ☐ c. he was crushed by his tractor.

2. When rancher Gary Skarda was thrown from his horse, he
   ☐ a. broke his back, his left arm, and his leg.
   ☐ b. broke his back and his right leg.
   ☐ c. broke his pelvis, his hip, and some ribs.

3. Singer Lyle Lovett and his uncle were injured by a
   ☐ a. bull that was out-of-control.
   ☐ b. crazed horse.
   ☐ c. runaway tractor.

4. According to the story, one survey says that ranching
   ☐ a. is among the best-paying jobs in the United States.
   ☐ b. ranks high for stress-related diseases.
   ☐ c. is a field that has many job openings.

5. A blizzard in 1973 reduced Pat Litton's sheep herd from
   ☐ a. 23,000 to 15,000.
   ☐ b. 4,000 to 2,000.
   ☐ c. 2,000 to 800.

Score 5 points for each correct answer.

_____ **Total Score:** Recalling Facts

C Making Inferences

When you combine your own experiences and information from a text to draw a conclusion that is not directly stated in that text, you are making an inference. Below are five statements that may or may not be inferences based on information in the article. Label the statements using the following key:

C—Correct Inference   **F—Faulty Inference**

_____ 1. Ranching would be a safer job if ranchers didn't use any machinery.

_____ 2. If you like and respect animals, you are never really in any danger from them.

_____ 3. Someone who likes ranching would probably not be happy in an office job.

_____ 4. Ranchers have to be good at a variety of tasks.

_____ 5. Sheep that are newly sheared should be sheltered during cold weather.

Score 5 points for each correct answer.

_____ **Total Score**: Making Inferences

D Using Words Precisely

Each numbered sentence below contains an underlined word or phrase from the article. Following the sentence are three definitions. One definition is closest to the meaning of the underlined word. One definition is opposite or nearly opposite. Label those two definitions using the following key. Do not label the remaining definition.

C—Closest   **O—Opposite or Nearly Opposite**

1. Everywhere a rancher looks, <u>potential</u> hazards loom.

    _____ a. not likely ever to happen

    _____ b. life-changing

    _____ c. possible

2. Beyond the dangers posed by equipment, ranchers often must spray their fields with <u>toxic</u> pesticides.

    _____ a. harmless

    _____ b. poisonous and deadly

    _____ c. foul-smelling

3. For example, diseases can <u>decimate</u> their herds.

    _____ a. confuse a large part of

    _____ b. kill a large part of

    _____ c. protect a large part of

4. A <u>significant</u> drop in market price can wipe out an entire year's profit in a single keystroke.

    _____ a. important, critical

    _____ b. minor or meaningless

    _____ c. steady

5. Young people are not <u>exempt</u> from having strong emotional ties to ranching.

_____ a. free from a rule or responsibility

_____ b. made to feel blame

_____ c. restricted or bound to

_____ Score 3 points for each correct C answer.

_____ Score 2 points for each correct O answer.

_____ **Total Score**: Using Words Precisely

Enter the four total scores in the spaces below, and add them together to find your Reading Comprehension Score. Then record your score on the graph on page 149.

Score	Question Type	Lesson 12
_____	Finding the Main Idea	
_____	Recalling Facts	
_____	Making Inferences	
_____	Using Words Precisely	
_____	**Reading Comprehension Score**	

Author's Approach

Put an X in the box next to the correct answer.

1. What is the author's purpose in writing this article?
☐ a. to convey a mood of sadness
☐ b. to describe the dangers and rewards of ranching
☐ c. to tell what happens when animals go out of control

2. From the statements below, choose the one that you believe the author would agree with.
☐ a. Successful ranchers must be creative and practical.
☐ b. Almost anyone could be good at ranching.
☐ c. Successful ranchers prefer to use only traditional methods.

3. The author tell this story mainly by
☐ a. retelling experiences from several ranchers' lives.
☐ b. describing several events from other sources.
☐ c. describing events in the order they happened.

4. In this article, "A significant drop in market price can wipe out an entire year's profit in a single keystroke" means
☐ a. If ranchers can't sell what they produce, they might not make a profit.
☐ b. One simple mistake at the computer can prevent ranchers from making a profit.
☐ c. If the price of what ranchers are selling goes down, they might not make a profit that year.

_____ Number of correct answers

Record your personal assessment of your work on the Critical Thinking Chart on page 150.

CRITICAL THINKING

Summarizing and Paraphrasing

Put an X in the box next to the correct answer.

1. Read the statement about the article below. Then read the paraphrase of that statement. Choose the reason that best tells why the paraphrase does not say the same thing as the statement.

   Statement: Nothing can persuade Pat Litton to leave her farm—not drought, floods, blizzards, or accidents—because ranching is her life.

   Paraphrase: Even though Pat Litton lost her husband and her son to ranch accidents, lost much of her sheep and cow herds to a blizzard, and was set back by droughts and floods, she still says that she will never stop ranching because it is what she does.

   ☐ a. Paraphrase says too much.

   ☐ b. Paraphrase doesn't say enough.

   ☐ c. Paraphrase doesn't agree with the statement.

2. Below are summaries of the article. Choose the summary that says all of the most important things about the article but in the fewest words.

   ☐ a. Hazards from machinery, animals, and weather make ranching dangerous, but ranchers still love it.

   ☐ b. Most people would find ranching to be an unusual thing to do, but many ranchers could not see themselves doing anything else with their lives.

   ☐ c. Out-of-control horses and bulls present a real danger to ranchers, as shown by the accidents that happened to Gary Skarda, Lyle Lovett, and Lyle's uncle.

   _____ Number of correct answers

   Record your personal assessment of your work on the Critical Thinking Chart on page 150.

Critical Thinking

Follow the directions provided for questions 1 and 3. Put an X next to the correct answer for the other questions.

1. For each statement below, write O if it expresses an opinion or write F if it expresses a fact.

   _____ a. It is hard to understand how ranchers can still enjoy ranching, since their jobs are quite dangerous.

   _____ b. Occasionally, even an animal that a rancher knows well can do something unexpected.

   _____ c. While trying to help his uncle, Lyle Lovett was attacked by a bull.

2. From the information in paragraph 6, you can predict that

   ☐ a. Lyle Lovett will probably become a rancher.

   ☐ b. Lyle Lovett will be nervous around angry bulls.

   ☐ c. Lyle Lovett's uncle will quit ranching.

3. Choose from the letters below to correctly complete the following statement. Write the letters on the lines.

   On the positive side, _____, but on the negative side _____.

   a. ranchers seem to be unusual people, in some ways

   b. ranchers must deal with dangerous problems every day

   c. ranching is a satisfying way of life

4. What was the cause of Gary Skarda's 22 days in the hospital?

   ☐ a. Skarda was run over by his own all-terrain vehicle.

   ☐ b. Skarda was trampled by a herd of bulls.

   ☐ c. Skarda's horse threw him hard.

CRITICAL THINKING

5. How is this article on ranching related to the theme of *Mavericks*?

☐ a. Ranchers often work on property that has been in the family for years.

☐ b. Ranchers must face dangers as a part of their job.

☐ c. Ranchers love their way of life and wouldn't change anything about it.

_____ Number of correct answers

Record your personal assessment of your work on the Critical Thinking Chart on page 150.

Personal Response

What would you have done if, like Lyle Lovett, you were nearby when an angry bull attacked a friend or relative of yours?

_____

_____

_____

_____

Self-Assessment

One of the things I did best when reading this article was

_____

_____

_____

_____ .

I believe I did this well because

_____

_____

_____

_____

_____ .

Embedded Journalists

Writing from the Front Lines

Embedded journalists are paid to report the war as it happens. Sometimes being close to the action means they also are part of the action.

O n paper, being a journalist sounds relatively clear-cut. Your job is to seek the truth and report it. In real life, however, things are rarely as simple as they sound, especially in the case of embedded journalists. They are not soldiers, and yet they eat, sleep, and travel with military units. They don't carry guns, and yet they run the constant risk of being killed by enemy assailants. They aren't supposed to take sides, and yet they are sometimes asked to carry a U.S. soldier's ammunition or assist a medic in the field. They want to tell their readers the truth, and yet there is certain information they have promised not to reveal. When did this job become so complicated?

2   The modern-day complexities of reporting from a war zone developed in 2003, when the idea of the embedded journalist was conceived. Before that time, if you were a reporter and you wanted to cover a war, you became a war correspondent. Typically, this meant that you ventured into a hot spot to see what you could see, and then you sent reports back to hometown news organizations. Sometimes war correspondents uncovered important stories about a war; in other

cases, important stories went untold. The system changed profoundly in 2003 when the United States Department of Defense, working with major news organizations, came up with a plan to insert, or "embed," about 600 reporters into specific military units in Iraq. Regular journalists could still poke around on their own, but embedded journalists would have unprecedented access to the daily activities of U.S. troops. The government described it as "long-term, minimally restrictive access to U.S. air, ground, and naval forces." Acknowledging that media coverage shapes public opinion, the U.S. government declared itself eager to have reporters get the truth directly from the men and women in the field, instead of allowing America's enemies to "seed the media with disinformation and distortions."

3   Improved access does not come without a price, however. In return for their front-row view of the war, embedded journalists have to abide by certain rules. For example, they cannot carry personal firearms. They also cannot send any electronic transmissions without getting the unit commander's approval, and this approval may be withheld whenever a commander feels a transmission would compromise the unit's safety. An embedded journalist can be kept from the front lines if the commander believes the conditions there are too dangerous. Embedded journalists agree not to divulge information about battle preparations, troop movements, or the equipment and supplies that a unit is carrying. In all, the embedding agreement runs 13 single-spaced pages.

4   For some journalists, the ground rules have caused a problem. For one thing, there is the question of perspective. Since embedded journalists must stay with one unit, it may be hard for them to develop a broad view of the war. Another danger is that they may identify too closely with the troops in their unit, thus losing objectivity. Finally, there is the question of whether agreeing to the government's rules means giving away too much autonomy. As Army First Lieutenant Paul Rieckhoff put it, "In my opinion, if you're embedded, you've compromised some of your journalistic integrity. You can't objectively cover both sides when I'm [protecting you]."

5   Finally, there is this problem: even when embedded journalists try to live with the restrictions set by the government, they may sometimes step over the line. When they do, it is surprising how quickly they can become "disembedded." Cheryl Diaz Meyer, a photojournalist with the Marines Second Tank Battalion in Iraq, took a starkly compelling picture of Iraqi civilians being strip searched by Marines. Diaz Meyer won praise for her work, becoming the first Filipina to receive a Pulitzer Prize for Breaking News Photography. But according to the embedding agreement, she was not supposed to show the faces of any Iraqi detainees. Because she had violated that rule, she was removed from her unit and stripped of her embedded status.

6   A similar thing happened to American photojournalist named Zoliah. He was embedded in a Marine unit in Iraq when a suicide bomber struck. Zoliah took pictures of the aftermath, including some photos of the three Marines killed in the attack. Four days later, he posted these pictures on his blog. The government declared that he had broken the embedding agreement by revealing how much damage the enemy

U.S. Army private Aquilla Reed, a broadcast journalist, works with an Afghan army officer in Paktya Province in Afghanistan.

attack had done. Zoliah was promptly removed from his Marine unit, a move he felt was unfair. "You're a war photographer," he said, "but once you take a picture of what war is like then you get into trouble."

7   Despite the limitations, some journalists have found that the embedding arrangement works extremely well. They say that by sharing the dangers, uncertainties, and hardships of soldiers' daily life in a war zone, they gain a better understanding of war—an understanding that they are able to communicate to their audience back home. Susan Stevenson of the Atlanta *Journal-Constitution* declared that "from what a blinding sandstorm feels like to reporting how one of our embeds broke his unit's coffee pot, we're giving readers a better sense of the field." CBS journalist Jim Axelrod would agree. "I found embedding to be an extremely positive experience," he said. "We got great stories and they got very positive coverage."

8   Michael Kelly, editor at large for the *Atlantic Monthly*, also defended the embedding program. He wrote that a system that allows eyewitness war reporting, no matter how constrained, "has to produce a picture of war, and of the military that goes to war, truer and more complete than a system that seeks to deny eyewitness reporting." Kelly didn't just talk about embedded journalism. He actually left his desk to become embedded with the Army's 3rd Infantry Division in Iraq.

9   In March of 2003, Kelly was asked about the dangers he faced as an embedded journalist in a war zone. "There is some element of danger," he acknowledged, "but you're surrounded by an Army, literally, who is going to try very hard to keep you out of danger." Sadly, trying and succeeding are two very different things. A month after making that statement, Michael Kelly was riding in an Army vehicle when a firefight broke out. The driver of his vehicle swerved desperately to avoid the gunfire,

but in doing so he drove off the road into a canal, killing both himself and Michael Kelly. Kelly's death did not end the embedded journalist program; it merely reinforced the point that for embedded journalists, the only thing that is really clear-cut is danger. ✶

If you have been timed while reading this article, enter your reading time below. Then turn to the Words-per-Minute Table on page 147 and look up your reading speed (words per minute). Enter your reading speed on the graph on page 148.

Reading Time: Lesson 13

_____ : _____

Minutes   *Seconds*

A Finding the Main Idea

One statement below expresses the main idea of the article. One statement is too general, or too broad. The other statement explains only part of the article; it is too narrow. Label the statements using the following key:

M—Main Idea   **B—Too Broad**   **N—Too Narrow**

_____ 1. Trying to report on wars while embedded in military units is neither easy nor safe.

_____ 2. In 2003 the United States Department of Defense allowed war correspondents to be embedded into military units for the first time.

_____ 3. Today, war correspondents who are embedded into U.S. military units can learn important information but cannot always report it freely or protect themselves from danger.

_____ Score 15 points for a correct M answer.

_____ Score 5 points for each correct B or N answer.

_____ **Total Score**: Finding the Main Idea

B Recalling Facts

How well do you remember the facts in the article? Put an X in the box next to the answer that correctly completes each statement about the article.

1. The first place where war correspondents were embedded in U.S. military units was in
   ☐ a. Iraq.
   ☐ b. Vietnam.
   ☐ c. Afghanistan.

2. Embedded journalists need the commander's approval to
   ☐ a. talk to enlisted men and women.
   ☐ b. carry a soldier's ammunition.
   ☐ c. send electronic transmissions.

3. Cheryl Diaz Meyer was removed from her unit for
   ☐ a. photographing enlisted men and women.
   ☐ b. photographing the faces of Iraqi detainees.
   ☐ c. refusing to ask for the commander's approval.

4. An American photojournalist named Zoliah got into trouble by
   ☐ a. reporting his experiences in a blog.
   ☐ b. protesting the war in Iraq.
   ☐ c. posting pictures of Marines who were killed.

5. Michael Kelly was an editor at
   ☐ a. the *Atlantic Monthly*.
   ☐ b. CBS News.
   ☐ c. the Atlanta *Journal-Constitution*.

Score 5 points for each correct answer.

_____ **Total Score**: Recalling Facts

C Making Inferences

When you combine your own experiences and information from a text to draw a conclusion that is not directly stated in that text, you are making an inference. Below are five statements that may or may not be inferences based on information in the article. Label the statements using the following key:

C—Correct Inference   **F—Faulty Inference**

_____ 1. Sometimes, embedded journalists become confused about what they are allowed to do.

_____ 2. Today's embedded journalists are better writers than war correspondents used to be.

_____ 3. The U.S. Department of Defense thinks it is important to control what reporters reveal to their readers.

_____ 4. Everyone agrees that embedding journalists in military units is a good idea.

_____ 5. In a war zone, no one is really safe.

Score 5 points for each correct answer.

_____ **Total Score**: Making Inferences

D Using Words Precisely

Each numbered sentence below contains an underlined word or phrase from the article. Following the sentence are three definitions. One definition is closest to the meaning of the underlined word. One definition is opposite or nearly opposite. Label those two definitions using the following key. Do not label the remaining definition.

C—Closest   **O—Opposite or Nearly Opposite**

1. They don't carry guns, yet they run the constant risk of being killed by enemy assailants.

_____ a. protectors

_____ b. attackers

_____ c. leaders

2. Regular journalists could still poke around on their own, but embedded journalists would have unprecedented access to the daily activities of U.S. troops.

_____ a. never before known

_____ b. unwelcome

_____ c. familiar

3. Another danger is that they may identify too closely with the troops in their unit, thus losing objectivity.

_____ a. ability to think quickly

_____ b. ability to view things without emotion or bias

_____ c. tendency to judge based on feelings or opinions

4. Finally, there is the question of whether agreeing to the government's rules means giving away too much autonomy.

_____ a. reliance on someone else

_____ b. ability to express things clearly

_____ c. independence

5. "In my opinion, if you're embedded, you've <u>compromised</u> some of your journalistic integrity."

_____ a. advertised

_____ b. safeguarded

_____ c. endangered

_____ Score 3 points for each correct C answer.

_____ Score 2 points for each correct O answer.

_____ **Total Score:** Using Words Precisely

Enter the four total scores in the spaces below, and add them together to find your Reading Comprehension Score. Then record your score on the graph on page 149.

Score	Question Type	Lesson 13
_____	Finding the Main Idea	
_____	Recalling Facts	
_____	Making Inferences	
_____	Using Words Precisely	
_____	**Reading Comprehension Score**	

Author's Approach

Put an X in the box next to the correct answer.

1. The main purpose of the first paragraph is to

☐ a. show why embedding journalists is a bad idea.

☐ b. explain why embedding journalists is complicated.

☐ c. encourage readers to support the U.S. military efforts.

2. Choose the statement below that is the weakest argument for embedding journalists into military units.

☐ a. Embedding allows commanders to prevent reporters from leaking information affecting the unit's safety.

☐ b. Embedding allows journalists to get a true view of what a soldier goes through.

☐ c. Because journalists are not trained fighters, they are safer being apart from the military efforts.

3. What does the author imply by saying "In all, the embedding agreement runs 13 single-spaced pages"?

☐ a. The agreement is longer than one would expect.

☐ b. The agreement is not very clear.

☐ c. No one ever really read the agreement.

4. In this article, "Improved access does not come without a price, however" means

☐ a. embedding journalists costs quite a bit of money.

☐ b. embedded journalists give up some of their professional freedom.

☐ c. the price for embedding journalists is too high.

_____ Number of correct answers

Record your personal assessment of your work on the Critical Thinking Chart on page 150.

Summarizing and Paraphrasing

Put an X in the box next to the correct answer.

1. Choose the best one-sentence paraphrase for the following sentence from the article: "Because she had violated that rule, she was removed from her unit and stripped of her embedded status."

   ☐ a. Even though she had followed the rules, her embedded privileges were taken away.

   ☐ b. Embedded journalists who break the rules will suffer the consequences.

   ☐ c. She was no longer allowed to be embedded because she broke the rule.

2. Below are summaries of the article. Choose the summary that says all the most important things about the article but in the fewest words.

   ☐ a. War reporters can now be embedded into military units, a situation that is often complicated but that gives readers a close, personal look at war.

   ☐ b. Reporters embedded in military units must be careful about what they reveal to their readers, because if they aren't, the government might disembed them from their units.

   ☐ c. Embedding journalists into U.S. military units, though a fairly new idea, is now an accepted way of reporting about wars.

_____ Number of correct answers

Record your personal assessment of your work on the Critical Thinking Chart on page 150.

Critical Thinking

Put an X in the box next to the correct answer for questions 1 and 2. Follow the directions provided for the other questions.

1. Which of the following statements from the article is an opinion rather than a fact?

   ☐ a. For some journalists, the ground rules have caused a problem.

   ☐ b. In real life, however, things are rarely as simple as they sound, especially in the case of embedded journalists.

   ☐ c. Diaz Meyer won praise for her work, becoming the first Filipina to receive a Pulitzer Prize for Breaking News Photography.

2. From the article, you can predict that if embedded journalists break their agreement with the government,

   ☐ a. they will be disembedded quickly.

   ☐ b. the government will forgive them a few times.

   ☐ c. they will be allowed to stay embedded only if they have a good reason for breaking the rules.

3. Choose from the letters below to correctly complete the following statement. Write the letters on the lines.

   In the article, _____ and _____ are alike because they both ran into trouble following the government rules.

   a. Susan Stevenson

   b. Cheryl Diaz Meyer

   c. Zoliah

4. Think about cause-and-effect relationships in the article. Fill in the blanks in the cause-and-effect chart, drawing from the letters below.

Cause | Effect

Diaz Meyer showed faces of Iraqi detainees. _____

_____ He was disembedded.

Kelly's vehicle ran into a firefight. _____

a. He died in Iraq.

b. Zoliah posted a photo showing Marines killed in an attack.

c. She was removed from her unit.

5. Which paragraphs provide evidence that supports your answer to question 4?

_____

_____ Number of correct answers

Record your personal assessment of your work on the Critical Thinking Chart on page 150.

Personal Response

If I were the author, I would add or change

_____

_____

because

_____

_____

_____

Self-Assessment

A word or phrase in the article that I do not understand is

_____

and the word or phrase means

_____

_____

_____

_____

_____

CRITICAL THINKING

Delta Force

Under Cover and Out of Sight

U.S. soldiers from Delta Force and soldiers from Iraq get ready for an ambush mission near Hawijah, Iraq, in 2010.

Try to wrap your mind around this: one of America's premier counterterrorist units doesn't exist. At least, it doesn't *officially* exist. Called 1st Special Forces Detachment-Delta or simply Delta Force, this unit's mission is to combat terrorism at home and abroad. Its operations are so classified and so sensitive that no government or U.S. Army official will acknowledge its existence on the record. Still, Delta Force is real enough when it responds to a bombing, a kidnapping, or any other terrorist threat to the nation. For instance, Delta Force is credited with safely extracting hostages from a hijacked airplane in Thailand in 1980. The four terrorists involved were killed and all of the passengers freed. Delta Force is also credited with infiltrating enemy lines in Iraq in 1991. It located enemy missile sites, which allowed American fighter planes to move in and destroy them.

2   Delta Force began in 1977 in response to several high-profile terrorist attacks around the world. Colonel Charles Beckwith of the U.S. Army was given two years to organize a group of fighters capable of taking on any and all terrorist threats. The Operators Training Course guidelines summarized Delta Force's mission this way: "We were not just going in harm's way; we were going to charge down harm's throat, grab a handful of his guts, and turn him inside out."

3   Delta Force members, called "operatives," work in the most dangerous settings imaginable. They may be called in to rescue hostages in some remote location where backup is nonexistent. They may have to sneak through an enemy city to free civilians being held in inhumane conditions. In the course of a mission, they may have to rappel down the face of a tall building, swim a raging river, or hot-wire a car. Whatever the situation, the operatives are usually vastly outnumbered and facing an enemy that won't hesitate to mow them down.

4   As an example of the peril they face, consider Mogadishu, Somalia, in 1993. The city was in chaos, as competing warlords fought violently for control of the streets. United Nations peacekeeping forces had tried to bring humanitarian aid to the city but had failed. On October 3 a U.S. Army Black Hawk helicopter was shot down over Mogadishu. Stranded on the ground, its UN crew tried to stave off the mob of angry Somalis that surrounded them. Into this nightmare charged two Delta Force operatives. Armed only with their sniper rifles and their pistols, the operatives fought off the mob for hours. Although both men—Master Sergeant Gary Gordon

The Black Hawk helicopter is the U.S. Army's premier all-utility vehicle. This armored, artillery-loaded helicopter can lift an entire 11-person, fully-equipped infantry squad quickly in almost any conditions.

and Sergeant 1st Class Randy Shughart—were ultimately killed, their heroic actions saved the life of the helicopter pilot.

5   To do their job, Delta Force operatives often rely not just on skill and courage but also on secrecy. So while most military personnel are easy enough to spot with their standard "high and tight" haircuts and neatly pressed uniforms, Delta Force operatives blend in with the civilian population. They may change their hairstyle and clothes to conceal their real identities. They may also use the same weapons as the indigenous population, again with the intent of remaining inconspicuous. Delta Force even has its own special fleet of airplanes and helicopters with no military markings whatsoever.

6   In case you were wondering how you can sign up for Delta Force, the short answer is—you can't. Due to its extraordinarily high standards, potential candidates for Delta Force are selected by invitation only. Your chances improve if you can speak a non-Western language, since missions may be mounted in pockets of the globe where English, French, or Spanish won't be of any use. Beyond that, you need to be tough, strong, self-sufficient, and fearless. Most recruits come from other elite units, such as the Army Rangers. The average Delta Force candidate is 31 years old, has already logged 10 years of military service, and has above-average intelligence. If you are one of the select few who are invited to apply, you still have to go through a grueling 18-day selection course featuring psychological tests, physical hardship, and sleep deprivation. Some say that Delta Force recruits must be able to do 37 sit-ups and 33 push-ups in one minute, run 18 miles in the dark and cover 40 miles of steep terrain carrying a 45-pound pack. If you successfully pass this preliminary course, you then advance to the six-month Operators Training Course. This includes highly-specialized training in such essential skills as air assaults, covert operations, and high-speed driving.

7   One skill Delta Force operatives certainly must have is marksmanship. It is rumored that recruits have to demonstrate 100-percent accuracy in shooting from 600 yards. That is more than a third of a mile! As the training guidelines state, all recruits must have "the ability to shoot what we intended to shoot and nothing else." One shooting exercise is known as CQB, or Close Quarter Battle. Here you must successfully charge a building where mock terrorists are holding hostages, shoot and "kill" all the terrorists, and rescue the hostages without disturbing a hair on their heads.

8   While many Americans admire Delta Force, not everyone is pleased with their actions. Some critics argue that operatives go beyond legal bounds in carrying out their missions. They believe that Delta Force has more power and less accountability than any U.S. military outfit should have. Who, they ask, makes sure that operatives don't commit illegal or unethical acts in their determination to accomplish a mission? Still, the prevailing sentiment seems to be that Delta Force deserves our respect and gratitude. Delta Force operatives are seen as dedicated, highly trained professionals who have one of toughest jobs in the U.S. military. Many people whisper to themselves, "Spare me the details of what you had to do, but thank you for doing it." Regardless of your opinion about Delta Force, you can now forget absolutely everything you have just read about this elite force because, as you recall, *it doesn't officially exist!* ✳

If you have been timed while reading this article, enter your reading time below. Then turn to the Words-per-Minute Table on page 147 and look up your reading speed (words per minute). Enter your reading speed on the graph on page 148.

Reading Time: **Lesson 14**

_____ : _____
Minutes   *Seconds*

A Finding the Main Idea

One statement below expresses the main idea of the article. One statement is too general, or too broad. The other statement explains only part of the article; it is too narrow. Label the statements using the following key:

M—Main Idea   **B—Too Broad**   **N—Too Narrow**

_____   1.   Delta Force is a military unit whose members must meet high standards and are selected by invitation only.

_____   2.   Delta Force is an American unit that combats terrorism.

_____   3.   Delta Force is a U.S. counterterrorist unit whose highly skilled members operate anywhere in the world.

_____   Score 15 points for a correct M answer.

_____   Score 5 points for each correct B or N answer.

_____   **Total Score**: Finding the Main Idea

B Recalling Facts

How well do you remember the facts in the article? Put an X in the box next to the answer that correctly completes each statement about the article.

1.   Delta Force began in

☐   a.   1980.

☐   b.   1977.

☐   c.   1991.

2.   In 1993 two Delta Force members saved the life of a Black Hawk helicopter pilot in

☐   a.   Somalia.

☐   b.   Thailand.

☐   c.   Iraq.

3.   According to the article, candidates for Delta Force are

☐   a.   chosen from the Army Rangers.

☐   b.   selected by invitation only.

☐   c.   picked from applicants who can speak a non-Western language.

4.   The Operators Training Course lasts

☐   a.   18 days.

☐   b.   6 months.

☐   c.   9 months.

5.   CQB is the name of a training exercise and stands for

☐   a.   Crisis Quality Battle.

☐   b.   Crisis Quarter Barrage.

☐   c.   Close Quarter Battle.

Score 5 points for each correct answer.

_____   **Total Score**: Recalling Facts

C Making Inferences

When you combine your own experiences and information from a text to draw a conclusion that is not directly stated in that text, you are making an inference. Below are five statements that may or may not be inferences based on information in the article. Label the statements using the following key:

C—Correct Inference   F—Faulty Inference

_____ 1. Delta Force is a very small unit because so few people are able to meet its high standards.

_____ 2. Because so much secrecy surrounds Delta Force operations, the public may never know about all of them.

_____ 3. Delta Force operatives are aware that they may be asked to lay down their lives to save others during a mission.

_____ 4. Delta Force operations have always taken place outside of the United States.

_____ 5. Because Delta Force members receive so much training and learn so many secrets, they are never allowed to retire from the unit.

Score 5 points for each correct answer.

_____ **Total Score**: Making Inferences

D Using Words Precisely

Each numbered sentence below contains an underlined word or phrase from the article. Following the sentence are three definitions. One definition is closest to the meaning of the underlined word. One definition is opposite or nearly opposite. Label those two definitions using the following key. Do not label the remaining definition.

C—Closest   O—Opposite or Nearly Opposite

1. Delta Force is credited with safely <u>extracting</u> hostages from a hijacked airplane in Thailand.

_____ a. physically removing

_____ b. inserting

_____ c. rescuing

2. Delta Force operatives may also use the same weapons as the <u>indigenous</u> population.

_____ a. heavily armed

_____ b. foreign

_____ c. local

3. Operatives change their hairstyles and clothes with the intent of remaining <u>inconspicuous</u>.

_____ a. obvious

_____ b. well-groomed

_____ c. unnoticed

4. Most recruits come from other <u>elite</u> units.

_____ a. ordinary

_____ b. top-notch

_____ c. military

5. The Operators Training Course includes highly specialized training in such skills as <u>covert</u> operations.

_____ a. treacherous

_____ b. undercover

_____ c. unconcealed

_____ Score 3 points for each correct C answer.

_____ Score 2 points for each correct O answer.

_____ **Total Score**: Using Words Precisely

Enter the four total scores in the spaces below, and add them together to find your Reading Comprehension Score. Then record your score on the graph on page 149.

Score	Question Type	Lesson 14
_____	Finding the Main Idea	
_____	Recalling Facts	
_____	Making Inferences	
_____	Using Words Precisely	
_____	**Reading Comprehension Score**	

Author's Approach

Put an X in the box next to the correct answer.

1. The main purpose of the first paragraph is to

☐ a. introduce to the reader what Delta Force is and what Delta Force does.

☐ b. explain how Delta Force began.

☐ c. inform the reader about terrorism in the world.

2. Which of the following statements from the article best describes Delta Force operatives?

☐ a. They may be called in to rescue hostages in some remote location where back-up is nonexistent.

☐ b. Delta Force members, called "operatives," work in the most dangerous situations imaginable.

☐ c. Delta Force operatives are seen as dedicated, highly trained professionals who have one of the toughest jobs in the U.S. military.

3. In this article, "Many people whisper to themselves, 'Spare me the details of what you had to do, but thank you for doing it'" means

☐ a. People are grateful to Delta Force operatives and are willing to look the other way and not question the methods the operatives use.

☐ b. Many people are not interested in hearing what Delta Force operatives do.

☐ c. People do not have the time to listen to the details of a Delta Force mission but appreciate the work of the Delta Force operatives.

_____ Number of correct answers

Record your personal assessment of your work on the Critical Thinking Chart on page 150.

CRITICAL THINKING

Summarizing and Paraphrasing

Follow the directions provided for question 1. Put an X in the box next to the correct answer for the other questions.

1. Look for the important ideas in paragraphs 6 and 7 in the article. Summarize those paragraphs in one or two sentences.

   _____

   _____

   _____

2. Choose the best one-sentence paraphrase for the following sentence from the article: "One skill Delta Force operatives certainly must have is marksmanship."

   ☐ a. Delta Force operatives must receive training in shooting at targets.

   ☐ b. Members of Delta Force must be extremely skilled in shooting.

   ☐ c. Skill in shooting is the only skill Delta Force operatives must have.

3. Read the statement from the article below. Then read the paraphrase of that statement. Choose the reason that best tells why the paraphrase does not say the same thing as the statement.

   Statement: Operatives are usually vastly outnumbered and facing an enemy that won't hesitate to mow them down.

   Paraphrase: Brave operatives usually fight huge groups of well-armed foes that want to destroy them.

   ☐ a. Paraphrase says too much.

   ☐ b. Paraphrase doesn't say enough.

   ☐ c. Paraphrase doesn't agree with the statement.

_____ Number of correct answers

Record your personal assessment of your work on the Critical Thinking Chart on page 150.

Critical Thinking

Put an X in the box next to the correct answer for questions 1 and 2. Follow the directions provided for the other questions.

1. Which of the following statements from the article is an opinion rather than a fact?

   ☐ a. The average Delta Force candidate is 31 years old, has already logged 10 years of military service, and has above-average intelligence.

   ☐ b. On October 3, a U.S. Army Black Hawk helicopter was shot down over Mogadishu.

   ☐ c. Delta Force has more power and less accountability than any U.S. military outfit should have.

2. From the article, you can predict that if the critics of Delta Force have their way,

   ☐ a. some actions of Delta Force will be investigated to make sure they are legal.

   ☐ b. the training of operatives will be made easier than they are at present.

   ☐ c. the requirements for operatives will not be as strict as they have been.

3. Choose from the letters below to correctly complete the following statement. Write the letters on the lines.

   In the article, _____ and _____ are alike because they are skills taught to Delta Force operatives.

   a. air assaults

   b. high-speed driving

   c. first aid

4. Reread paragraph 2. Then choose from the letters below to correctly complete the following statement. Write the letters on the lines.

According to paragraph 2, _____ because _____.

a. the U.S. military wanted to be able to respond to terrorist acts

b. the Operators Training Course offered tough guidelines

c. Delta Force was begun

5. Which paragraph provides evidence that supports your answer to question 2?

_____

_____ Number of correct answers

Record your personal assessment of your work on the Critical Thinking Chart on page 150.

Personal Response

Would you recommend this article to other students? Explain.

_____

_____

_____

_____

_____

Self-Assessment

I'm proud of how I answered question _____ in the _____ section because

_____

_____

_____

_____

_____

_____

_____

_____

_____

CRITICAL THINKING

Bush Pilots

Tough Take-Offs, Rough Landings

Bush plane pilots in Alaska fly over hanging glaciers, between mountain peaks, and through freezing rain and mist without the help of air-traffic controllers. Most rely on a steady hand and sharp eyesight.

"Flying is the second greatest thrill known to man . . . Landing is the first!"   —*bush pilot humor*

Being a bush pilot is different from being a commercial jet pilot in two significant ways. First, the average bush pilot makes a lot less money than the average airline pilot. Second, the average bush pilot is a lot more likely to crash. A big reason for the higher accident rate is that jet pilots have at their disposal all sorts of sophisticated equipment, while bush pilots often have to rely on nothing more than their own seat-of-the-pants flying skills. George Conway of the National Institute for Occupational Safety and Health (NIOSH) says that the most common kind of accident for a bush pilot is a "controlled flight into terrain." That is a polite way of saying the plane is working perfectly fine, but the pilot suddenly loses visibility due to clouds or fog and he or she flies into a mountain—end of story.

2   The "bush" in bush pilot is a shorthand way of saying "wilderness." Bush pilots fly small, propeller-powered planes to remote places where commercial jet airlines can't or won't fly. Bush pilots fly into places without railroads, conventional airports, or adequate roads. You would find bush pilots